The Writing on the Wall

LYNNE REID BANKS

1981

CHATTO & WINDUS

LONDON

Published by
Chatto & Windus Ltd
40 William IV Street
London WC2N 4DF
*
Clarke, Irwin & Co. Ltd
Toronto

*British Library Cataloguing
in Publication Data*

Banks, Lynne Reid
  The Writing on the wall.
  I. Title
  823'.9'1F
  ISBN 0-7011-2568-3

2078
2

Printed in Great Britain by
Redwood Burn Ltd, Trowbridge and Esher

To the Ronders

1 · My Background

Well, *I* didn't know, did I. Well. I did know. I mean I did in a way.

My brother Vlady kept saying, "Didn't you see what he was up to? Can you swear you didn't guess?"

Well, I can tell a lie same as anybody, but swearing's something else. Swearing's like on the Bible. Mum used to make us put our hands on the Bible when she thought we were telling lies, and make us swear. Sean – my other brother – he could do it all right, but I never could. Never. I'd go all red and start to stammer. Honest to God, I thought I'd be struck dead. A bit of me still does.

So did I know, or didn't I?

I knew there was something fishy. That I knew. I may not be clever but I'm not daft. But then, you often break the law, don't you. Little ways I mean. Nicking sweets as a kid, and going on the tube without paying, and sneaking in to X films and pubs when you're under age – that's just silly, everyone does that, they shouldn't make such silly laws. Even my dad, that's so strict, breaks the law sometimes. Parking on the double yellow and that. Course, it's not his fault they spoilt trade by putting a double yellow outside his shop, and he's got to unload. Still, who knows what he gets up to when nobody's looking?

Of course I'm not saying what I did wasn't worse. But at the time I didn't think. That's why it came as such a shock when they all started going at me. At me, and at each other. That was the worst in a way. The rows inside the family. Over my head. Feeling it was my fault, just because I hadn't stopped to think. . . .

Well. I'd best start at the beginning.

You could say the real beginning was Dad and Mum meeting at the Polish Club in the war. Mum's Irish, so someone must have taken her there. The Poles were big heroes in those days. Dad's older than Mum – he's over sixty now. He was in Anders'

Army. Anders was a Polish general who got together some Poles who'd got out of Poland, to fight the Nazis.

And the ones stationed in London had their own club. Girls used to go there to dance with them. And Mum was Catholic, like Dad, and pretty in those days. Lots younger than Dad. Anyway, about five years after the war, they got married.

Dad got work in a shop. It wasn't what he could have got if only he'd spoken better English. He's got a brain, my dad has, but no ear for languages he says, and that was his big handicap.

Sometimes I'm a bit ashamed of the way he talks. Mum's Irish isn't so bad, it's less foreign. There were always lots of Irish families and kids around where we lived, but not so many foreigners. The kids used to tease me, say I was up the Pole and ask me if my dad used a po, seeing he came from Po-land. They only switched to sneering about the Irish when the IRA started up heavy again in the last few years, and the Irish jokes came in. *God*, I hate those Irish jokes! Nobody'd dare tell jokes like that about the blacks; you'd be had up by the Race Relations.

Anyhow, Mum and Dad worked hard and after a few years they moved to Acton where there's as many Polish people as Irish. They bought a big house on a big mortgage and took in lodgers until they'd filled the whole place up with their own kids. The first one died and Mum swore she'd never have another, and she didn't for quite a bit; but being Catholic she couldn't keep to it. After a few years she had Vladimir. He's twenty-four now. And then she had Sean, who's nineteen. That was one name for each country. Then came my big sister Mary. Then came me.

They christened me Teresa, but I wasn't having that. When I went to high school from middle school I changed it to Tracy. Mum and Dad didn't like it, they said it sounded cheap (they knew I'd got it out of *Fab* magazine). Besides, there's no saint called Tracy (and there's not going to be one, not if anyone's counting on me). But I'd made my mind up. I wouldn't answer when they spoke to me unless they called me Tracy. In the end even my little sister, Lily, gave in. Lily made five of us and Mum drew the line at that. I don't know how you draw the line when you go to confession every week, but this time she did stick to it.

So I grew up in this big house with a big garden where Dad grows vegies and Mum hangs out rows and rows of clean washing. Soon as Lily was in school, Mum threw out the last lodger and went back to work. Even though Dad had his own shop by this time. It's a Polish delicatessen on the High Street – lots of different sausages, and breads, and shelves full of Krakus products. Every Pole in the district shops there. Once, Dad was making an appeal for kids in Cambodia and he put the notice beside the box in Polish. An English woman complained. She said, "Can't I contribute? This is England, you know." Dad misses Poland. He hates the government there and couldn't go back, but he's still homesick.

We were all right. Ups and downs, same as any family, but all right. Funny, I suppose, Mum and Dad coming from different countries and that, and the age difference, but getting on so well. Must be the religion. They're ever so different, aside from that. *How* different I didn't know till recently.

Well, so that's my background. As to what I look like, that's a family joke. Every kid in the family takes after Mum – even Vlady, in looks – except me. That's why Dad calls me his Polish daughter. I'm the only fair-haired, round-faced one. I've got a big forehead and a balloony mouth and these sort of long, wide-apart eyes. All the others are either very dark like Mum, or red-haired like Gran, and have green eyes. My eyes are pale blue with dark blue rims. Dad says I'm beautiful, but then he would. I'm his favourite.

I *was*. Don't know about from now on.

I'm sixteen. I left school last July. No tears, you can bet; I'd been aching to get out since I was fourteen. Couldn't seem to learn any more. Well, I haven't got my dad's head. None of us has, saving Vlady. Talking of favourites, he's my favourite brother. But I'm not his favourite sister. He thinks I'm stupid. Though he used to help me a bit with my schoolwork when he had the patience. Maths and that I never could do, never got the hang of it somehow. English was my best subject. I've got this good imagination, I could always invent stuff. Trouble was my spelling.

Once I wrote this smashing story about a girl who gets mixed up with a black boy (I fancied one myself a bit at the time). I just wrote and wrote. I wrote half the night, and my writing got ropier and my spelling got weirder, but I was carried away. I couldn't be bothered to copy all that out again of course, so next day I handed it in. Miss Nelson, my teacher, always gave me good marks before, but this time do you know what she wrote on the bottom? *One out of ten*. "One for effort," she said but the spelling ruined it.

I never tried for her after that. I used to write bits at home sometimes, but I never did another good thing for her. Cow.

So when I finally left I hadn't even taken one O-level. I took four CSE's because they made me, but the only one I think I might've got is History. Because I happened to've read a book about Henry VIII after that thing about him on the telly, and one of the main questions was about the Tudors. So I just wrote lots of detail. Like how when Anne Boleyn (wife number two) was topped on Tower Green, Henry was out hunting in Richmond Park. They fired off the guns like they always did for a royal execution, and instead of feeling sorry, Henry shouted out: "The deed is done! Uncouple the hounds and away!" What a sod, eh? Anyhow I bet they'll like me knowing that and some other stuff. So maybe I'll get a good grade; you never know.

Not that that'll get me a good job. I didn't even try for any of the other subjects. Dad wasn't half upset, but I couldn't help it, could I? I hated school. Such a row going on all the time. How could you listen even if you wanted to? Not that I didn't join in sometimes. Well, you have to, you can't help yourself when everybody's doing it.

Anyhow I wasn't panting to get a job right away. I wanted a bit of a rave-up first. I got it, too. And now look at me!

I had this boyfriend. Kevin, his name was. This bit's hard to tell. First because I have to go back to before I left school. Second because if I'm going to tell the story right, I have to imagine myself back into fancying him, before all the mess.

Mind you, he was good looking. The haircut suited him, and you can't say that about a lot of them. You have to have a good shape to your head, and flat ears and that. And a good profile. And not too many spots. Funny how many punks and skinheads are very thin, and have spots.

Kevin had a skinhead cut on top, and at the sides he grew it long and did it up with black shoe-polish to make it stand in spikes. And after school he'd wear the whole bit, bondage trousers, pins in his ears, the lot. Some of his mates copied him, and I got to like some of their gear, and the whole look. It just about showed what I thought of school. So one night I got Mary to give me a hair-cut in our room, and she helped me dye my hair (what was left of it) pink and white. She kept egging me on to try the green, but I reckoned Mum and Dad would have enough of a fit as it was. And I wasn't wrong.

When I came down to breakfast next morning I put a scarf over my head, but Vlady caught a glimpse of pink tuft and pulled it off (the scarf, not the tuft). You should've heard the row. Mum screamed and Lily had hysterics laughing. The boys simply went mad. They jeered and pointed and fell all over the table. Sean went over backwards in his chair and his big feet sent a plate of bacon flying. Dad? Dad just sat there looking at me. Then he got up and walked out.

My form-teacher started creating before you could turn round that morning. He must've been spying as I walked across the yard.

"What's the idea, Tracy? Gone over to the barbarians?"

"Dunno what you're on about," I said.

"You look idiotic. And ugly. I don't allow outrageous cult-fads in my class." He's a fanatic of course. At least about the girls. (He turns a blind eye on the boys, that's how Kev got away with it.) He won't stand for high heels or earrings or anything. He even tried to stop us using make-up!

I got a bit stroppy next off, and told him it was none of his business. So I got sent to Mr Breasley. That was our head. And he gave me his ultimatum.

No waiting for it to grow out, nothing like that. "You're not going to class looking like a hooligan," he said. "You're going to Woolworth's or wherever you got that rubbish you've used on your hair. If they're selling pink in bottles they're selling blonde in bottles. You can dye it back to its natural colour."

And that's what I had to do. Except I had to use brown to drown out the pink, which upset Dad almost worse because now I didn't look so Polish any more. And in case you think I was scared of old Breeze-up, I wasn't. Believe me. It was my dad. I wasn't having him looking at me for weeks and not saying anything, the way he had at breakfast.

Still, I didn't do it right away. I wanted Kevin to see it first. So I hung around till break, and when he came out with his mates, Cliff and Darryl, I signalled him from the school gate. And they all strolled over, goggling at my hair.

As much as Dad and Breeze-up didn't reckon it, of course, Kev did. I suppose he guessed right off I'd done it for him. He'd never touched me before, except to punch my arm and that, like all the boys do when they want you to notice them. But now he put his hand on my head and rubbed my short hair.

He did it a bit rough. Not like in that old film where the girl had her hair shaved and it grew back into little short curls and the hero (Gary Cooper I think it was; anyhow one of those old stars who's dead now) kind of strokes it, gentle, and it pops up between his fingers. Fair brought me out in goosebumps, that did. More than all the rolling about in the raw you get now.

Anyhow, Kev gave my head this hard rub which nearly broke my neck, and Cliff and Darryl wanted to have a go too, but Kev stuck out his elbows and kept them off me. I reckoned that was a good sign. Then I told him about old Breeze-up and how I had to dye it back, and Kev said, "Don't worry, girl, it's the cut I like. What you do it with, a Polish razor?" (When they call anything Polish, it means it doesn't work. I'm used to it. Just so Dad doesn't hear.)

"My sister cut it with Mum's sewing shears," I said.

They all hooted. "What you laughing at?" I yelled.

"Tracy's been sheared! Where's your fleece then? I want Tracy's wool to make my winter woollies!" Bunch of clowns, jumping about. . . . But Kev just stood there looking at me and I knew he really liked my hair. I felt sick at having to go back to being dull and normal.

Didn't matter though, as it turned out, because even after I'd done it he still fancied me. We were in the same class and he used to pass me notes. They were never anything private because of course everyone had a peep, didn't they, when they were passing them. They were usually just something like, *Why don't you wash your neck sometimes?* or *Stop listening so hard, you'll get ereacke.* (His spelling was worse than mine.) But I reckoned he wouldn't be writing notes in the first place if he didn't like me. He didn't to any of the other girls. Even Karen, and all the boys were after her.

Karen and me'd been pals since we started high school. She's ever so lucky. Her dad works as a commissionaire for the BBC up Western Avenue and she goes there sometimes and even sees some of the shows. And she can go in the staff canteen, where there's telly stars all over the place. Just imagine – Esther Rantzen and Terry Scott and all that lot, queueing up with their trays like anyone else. Once she sat at the same table with Larry Grayson and he passed her the salt! I kept on at her to take me, but she never would.

That's one advantage she has. She's got another. And that's something she does share around. I don't want to be catty, or gossip. But I was surprised that Kev never seemed to fancy her. And glad. Because she's dead sexy. I won't say she's anybody's. But she's not exactly nobody's, either.

2 · Kev

Dad didn't like Kev.

I knew he wouldn't. Karen says your dad never likes the boys you go out with, he never thinks they're good enough. But I think with Kev it was more than that. Dad just took one look at his hair-spikes and his Dayglo socks and his brass-studded collar, and he sort of closed up.

Not that he said much. Mum's different. She said plenty. But then she says her mind about all my friends, boys and girls. She never says she doesn't like them, she just criticises them to death. With Karen, it was: "Why does a girl with such pretty eyes want to paint round them like that for?" and "She'll grow old with bunions, tiptupping along on those silly heels!" As for Kev, it was: "He looks like the Statue of Liberty with that mad hairdo" and "If he spends so much on his boots, it's a pity he can't buy some polish to go on them." She asked about his family. She always does. "Is his dad in a job? Does his mum go out to work?" She didn't ask if they're Catholics. Everyone who goes to our school is.

That's why I never brought that black boy home, nor let them see me walking with him. Not because he was black. Because he was Rastafarian. For Mum, that'd be the same as pagan.

So when Kev finally asked me out, I didn't tell them the truth. I said I was going to the pictures with Karen. Dad always wants to know what I'm going to, to make sure it's not an X. Even now, he does it. Little does he know I've been going to X's since I was fourteen – I was always tall for my age.

I told him we were going to see *Julia*. My dad never goes to films – never – but he knows all about what's on because he reads the crits and watches Barry Norman on the box. I knew I was on to a good thing with this *Julia* because Dad's got this hang-up about the war and the Nazis. He's always trying to tell us about how horrible the Germans were and what they did and all that, till I'm sick of it. So when I said "Julia" he was pleased.

"I'd like you should see that," he said. "It's a truth story." Dad never has managed to get "true" and "truth" right. For instance, the whole family says "to say the true" instead of "to tell the truth". It started as a tease, like "Can I help you somesing?" which is another of his phrases.

So it was all systems go, though Dad did get a bit of a funny look in his eye when I came down in all my gear that evening.

He never liked me in my punk gear. Not that he ever really made a fuss because he says teen-age is dressing-up time and there's no harm in it. But still, I could tell that just as he'd hated my short, pink-and-white hair, he hated my red cheeks and eye-shadow and my green lips and the silver and black stars I'd stuck on. And my tight pants, half pink and half black, and high heels, and satin jockey-jacket that I'd picked up in a jumble sale.

"Like that, you go out with your girlfriend?" Dad asked.

"Sure, why not?"

"And would it spoil your fun if I said, you look better when you don't chew gum?"

"Who cares how I look?"

"I do," he said.

"All I care is that I look *right*," I said.

"Does 'right' mean 'horrible' nowadays?"

"When you're a punk, it does."

"Do you look horrible to another punk?"

I hope not, I thought, thinking of Kev. But aloud I just said, "You wouldn't understand, Dad. I'm off now."

"Be home early. I wait up."

No use telling him not to – he always did. So I went out, and round the corner I met Kev. He was in his full gear as well, and he didn't look horrible to me, which answered Dad's question. He said, "You look great," and I said, "You too," and he rubbed my hair and told me we were going into the West End.

Kev didn't often have much money. His dad's out of work most of the time, and the family lives on Security, even though I heard his mum goes out cleaning and gets paid cash. I suppose that's what his dad uses to back horses, because sometimes he wins and then Kev's in funds for a bit.

We had a Macdonald's Kingsize and chips, and one of their stand-your-straw-straight-up milkshakes, and then we went to one of those pleasure arcades near Piccadilly and played the games. Kev was always at the one in our local chippy, but with that one you don't get money if you win, you just get a free go. These you could win at. Kev gave me five 10p's and I played till I lost them, which wasn't long, and then watched him play. He was lucky. He won his second go, and after that he kept on, win, lose, win, for about an hour. He lost it all in the end, but we'd had a good cheap evening and before we left he stood me a go at the one like we used to play with at fairgrounds, the crane that comes down and grabs something and drops it down the hole. Only it usually doesn't pick up anything. But it was our lucky night. It picked up a glittery hair-slide, like a butterfly. Except that when I reached up to put it in my hair, of course I found I hadn't got anything to pin it to. So we laughed and I put it in my pocket.

Then it was still early so we walked about the streets and looked at the porn-show pictures. I didn't like them much. I suppose it's my upbringing. Mum'd never let us see anything like that when we were little. I mean she'd never let the *Sun* in the house for instance, and anything that looked rude, on telly, say, she'd have it switched off before you could blink. Karen says her mum let her see her in the bath, but my mum, when she's in there she doesn't even splash much in case it should make us imagine things. So when I see mags and that, and these displays in Soho, well, I get embarrassed.

But I wasn't going to let Kev see how I felt. *He* seemed to think it was all perfectly natural. But then he often comes up West so I suppose he's used to it. I wanted to ask if he'd ever been to one of the shows but I was afraid he'd say yes and tell me what was in them. I wanted to know, in a way, but not from him.

Then I reckoned it was time to get home, but Kev had other ideas.

"I got a mate's we could go to," he says. "For a drink."

Well, I'm not daft. I mean, he was nice and all that, and I fancied him, but they all try it on, don't they. Mary's told me. And Karen. With Karen they didn't even have to try too hard. And she's not the only one in our class. Couple of girls I know had it away at fourteen. One of them had to leave school. . . . That was what kept me off it. Partly. Partly it was

Dad and Mum, and my family and all that. And. . . . Well. Confession. I never could see myself telling Father Gilligan a thing like that. Anyway I didn't fancy anyone enough. Till Kev.

Still, when he said about going to his mate's I said, "No. Let's go to a disco." But he'd got no more money. We were hanging about outside Leicester Square tube by now and it was getting cold. The wind was blowing the litter along the pavement. There were a couple of drunks coming out of a pub, and some other funny types I didn't like the looks of.

"Come on, Kev," I said, tugging his arm. "Let's go home."

"Oh all *right*," he said and walked away from me down the tube, leaving me to follow as best I could through the crowd.

We had a fair walk from Acton station. He walked a bit ahead of me most of the way and didn't talk. I could see he was pissed off but I didn't know why, if it was something I'd done or just a mood. I felt miserable, trailing along after him. Then I remembered Karen saying they always act sullen if you don't give in to them. Like blackmail.

Still, I wanted him to cheer up. So when he stopped, on the big railway bridge, I pulled myself up beside him and we hung over, waiting for a train to go under us. One did. Kev said, "D'you ever drop anything?"

"What?"

"Over the bridge."

"On to the train, you mean?"

"Yeah."

"Course not! Whatever for?"

"See it bounce off."

"That's just thick. Could hurt someone."

"It only hits the roof."

"What does? What do you throw?"

"Coke tins. Stones. Any old rubbish."

I didn't say anything. I thought it was stupid. But Mary says you have to realise, boys do daft things sometimes, to let off steam.

"Well?" he said in this sort of taunting way he had, as if he was giving me a dare. "What's wrong?"

"Nothing," I said quickly. "What'll we throw, though? Nothing here."

He looked all round, and we both spotted it at once – a spray can, lying in the gutter. Kev pounced on it. He gave it a shake.

"It's half-full," he said.

"What is it, Windolene?"

"No. It's paint-spray."

"What colour?"

"White."

I knew what he was going to do just before he thought of it. He pointed it at me and started towards me, grinning.

"Don't you dare!" I screamed, half-laughing but a bit scared. That stuff won't come off.

"I liked your hair with a bit of white in it," he said. I backed away, my hands over my hair.

"Kev, don't! I mean it!" But he was still coming at me. I had to think, quick, of something more exciting for him to spray than me. "Listen, I tell you what! Let's spray something on the bridge."

That stopped him. "Like what?"

"I dunno, anything you like! Then Monday when we go past to school we can look at it and know we wrote it. It'll stay there for ever."

He looked at the wall of the bridge. It was dark brick, nothing on it, just asking for some mark or other. Like fresh snow asks to be walked on.

He grinned at me. Then he suddenly handed me the tin.

"Here. You do it. Then we'll throw it over when the next train comes."

Sometimes you do something because you don't know what else to do. You get caught up. I'm telling about this because it was the beginning. The first time I did something I didn't want to do because Kev kind of pushed me into it. I didn't want to spray words on that wall and I didn't want to throw the tin on the train. It was daft. So why did I do it then? I don't know. I wish I did.

I couldn't think of a thing to write at first. I just stood there.

Kev said, "Write your initials and mine in a love-heart."

I looked at him. His face was in shadow, just outside the lamp circle. Did he mean it? Or was he laughing at me, for being a girl and having silly, romantic thoughts? "Then everyone'll see," I said.

He threw his head back and roared, a great guffaw.

"You didn't really think I'd let you? You silly cow, I'd half kill you if you did that!"

That hurt me. It made me mad, too. First sulking because I wouldn't go to a strange flat with him, and now calling me names. So I put my finger on the spray button and wrote

KEV B IS A BASTERD

"D'you like that better?" I asked him.

He looked at the words, and looked at me. The second I finished doing it, I was sorry. I was scared, but I was sorry too. It looked awful, white on black in the lamp light, there for the world to see. I'd have given anything not to have done it. I would now. Why did I? Temper, that's all. I've got a terrible, mad temper sometimes.

"You need doing up, you do," he said. His voice was all quiet and threatening. I thought he might really hurt me, and I felt quite weak with fear for a minute.

"You shouldn't have called me a cow," I said. My voice came out all breathy.

"That's there for good," he said, pointing to the words. "I shan't forget that in a hurry."

Just then we heard a train coming. "Come on!" I said, quick, to distract him. "Get ready!"

He hesitated, but then he did go to the wall and pull himself up. I got up beside him, and we leaned over.

"I should throw *you* over, you know that," he said, over the roar of the train. "But I'll think of some other way to get back at you. Go on – throw the can down."

The train roared under us and I held the empty tin over the edge. But I couldn't drop it. I just couldn't. In the end Kev gave me a thump on the wrist, and the tin hit the train roof, bounced off, and then fell alongside the track.

The bridge trembled under our stomachs. I felt excited. Almost sick with it somehow. We dropped back down onto the pavement, and then Kev grabbed me. I got a fright – I thought he was still mad. The train was still roaring, or maybe it was just a noise in my ears. And I was still shaking after the bridge had stopped. Then Kev kissed me on the mouth. I didn't know if I liked it or not. It was scary, especially coming right after he'd been so angry. As if that hard, passionate kiss was a punishment. But I wanted him to do it again. I wanted, in a way, to do it all again, just to get that shaky, dizzy feeling, to hear that roaring in my head.

3 · Dutch Treat

After that night I went out with Kev every weekend. It got very tricky, making up things to tell Dad. I soon used up all the war films, for a start. I let it go on for three or four weeks and then I knew I'd have to tell him it was Kev, not Karen. Don't ask me why I had to tell him. Half the time I don't *know* why I do things. If it's not Kev or Vlady or someone outside myself pushing me, it's something inside. I just couldn't go on making things up. Imagination or no imagination.

One night after school I left the telly and went into the kitchen. Our kitchen's our eating room too. Mum calls it the dining-room even though the stove and sink and that's staring her in the face. I think if Mum had one wish, about the house anyway, she'd ask for a separate room to eat in. We've got a room that could be it, but it's Vlady's room. Dad insisted, when he saw Vlady's got brains and needed a quiet place to study.

Dad was sitting at the table reading a Polish paper. He looked up as I came in and gave me a smile. He still looks foreign. I don't notice it, but Karen said once. Something about his lips. A bit balloony, like mine. Not that I care.

I was trying to be casual. Karen says, when she's got to do something – like tell the teacher she hasn't done her project or face her mum about something – she always practises it first. Of course that's because she's stuck on acting and that. She calls it "rehearsing". I can't rehearse. I don't like thinking of things ahead. If I've got to do them, I go and do them. What's the use thinking what could happen? It's like going through it twice.

All right, so I sat down opposite Dad and said straight out: "I've been going out with Kevin, not Karen."

"I thought so," he said, quiet. And went back to his Polish paper.

"You're not cross?"

"Not now you've told me," he said. He looked as if he was reading, but after a minute he put out his hand, under the edge of the paper, and left it lying on the table. I put my hand into it and he gave me a squeeze. He put down the paper and smiled at me.

"Tell me the rest," he said.

Well. *All* the rest, the necking and that, I wasn't about to tell him, I mean I couldn't. But I told him we'd been up West and I told him about the one film we really did see, which was *Love at First Bite*, about this vampire.

I always know when Dad's disappointed in me. His eyes kind of go sad. Sometimes when he gets this sad, droop-eyed look, I feel like screaming. How can I be different than I am, how can I be more what he wants, clever and that? I can't help not liking the books and films and stuff he wants me to like, I can't help liking pop music and girls' magazines. And Kev.

"Does he take good care of you?" he asked.

"Course he does."

"You don't do any bad?"

"Oh Dad. . . ."

"Oh Dad," he copied me. He sighed. He's got this deep sigh, like he had all the world's worries. Mum says it's because of all the things he saw in the war when he was young. It made him sort of always a little bit sad underneath. "Expecting the worst from people," Vlady says.

Vlady's very sharp about people. Once when I had one of my moods and sulked round the house for a day, and shouted at Dad, Vlady got hold of me. He pulled me into his room, the one that ought to be the dining-room, and locked the door. "You listen to me," he said, fierce. "Just stop it or I'll give you something to sulk about! Dad's had enough in his life. He deserves some happiness from his family. We got to make it up to him." I was much younger then and nobody'd told me anything, so I sulked back at him, "Make what up?" So then he told me. All Dad's family was killed by the Nazis in a camp in north Poland called Stutthoff. Vlady told me the whole thing, about the ovens and the gas chamber and that.

Course I'd heard something. There's kids at school even make jokes about it, but I thought it was just the Jews. Vlady said lots of the clever people in Poland were killed too. Dad's father was a teacher, so they killed him because they thought he might make trouble, teach against them and that.

24

I was upset – course I was. But I didn't want to think about it. Still, I was nicer to Dad after that, for a while anyway. I do try with my moods but sometimes I can't help it.

Anyway, so we were sitting at the table and I suddenly wanted to tell Dad everything, only I couldn't because it would make him more disappointed. He'd be sure to think it was wrong to paint on the wall, and I know what he thinks of pinball machines or any kind of gambling. It makes him sick. He says it's for idiots with nothing in their heads, or for idlers with nothing better to do. My dad's a Catholic, of course, but Vlady says his real religion is work. He thinks the worst sin is not to work. Maybe that's why he didn't like Kev, because his dad's always out of work. Not that that's Kev's fault, now is it?

The only thing he said, after that big sigh, was: "You're too young to go out with a boy. That's my view. But if I try to stop you, you will do something foolish. I will have to trust you, my little girl. Because *him* I don't trust, not so far as I could throw the House of Parliament." I tried to take my hand away but he held on and smiled his sad Polish smile into my eyes, and then he added, "Don't go to the West End. It is a bad place at night. Tell me where you want to go and I take you in the car. I gladly take you, and I fetch you back if you phone me."

Of course that would have killed all the fun so from then on I told Kev I wanted just to go into Ealing or Hammersmith to the films or for a Wimpy or sometimes to a pub. We were too young to drink in pubs, but in some areas they're not too fussy. We sometimes spent a whole evening in a pub when Kev was skint. It was boring in a way but I wanted to be with him so I had to do what he did.

We did a lot of necking now. I always felt funny about it, and I always confessed it (when I didn't forget to go – Mum usually didn't let me forget). Father Gilligan didn't make too much of it, but he always said I should be careful not to let it go any further. Kev acted like he wanted it to go further, but I used to hold his hands away.

Once I said, "Do you tell your mates about this?"

"Course not," he said, but I wasn't so sure. Karen says they all talk about it. And I thought Darryl and Cliff and that lot had started looking at me kind of smirky at school. Made me feel like hitting them in the face.

And then there was Karen.

If you ask me, Karen was a bit jealous. She and I had been together a lot till Kev came into my life. And then she had this idea that boys only want one thing and that unless you give it to them they'll push off to some girl who will. So when I told her I didn't let Kev do more than neck a bit, she didn't believe me. It upset all her ideas.

"He must be getting it from someone else," she said.

"No he's not, he doesn't go with other girls."

"That's what he tells you!"

"That's what I know."

She thought a bit and looked at me sideways. "What if I told you he was getting it from me?"

"I'd say you was a liar," I said. But my face had gone all cold. Not that I believed her for a second, but I was shocked she'd try to pull a thing like that when we were supposed to be friends.

Straight off she saw she'd gone too far.

"I was just kidding," she said, quick.

"If that's a joke, you better go and buy a new joke-book," I said. And I walked away.

I felt bad, though. That's the trouble with people you like. *They* may be in the wrong, but *you* feel bad after. You want to make it up but how can you? It's up to them to make a move. Karen didn't. She's like that. So I felt miserable.

Kev met me after school. "What you looking so down for?" he asked. "You ought to be happy. Another two weeks and we'll be out of this hole."

He meant school. It was the middle of June, our last-ever term. Yeah, I should have felt happy. But "to say the true" I was more scared. I didn't know what I was going to do with my life. Kev didn't either, but he wasn't bothered. Took a lesson from his dad. *He* wasn't afraid of being out of work, he was used to it. So Kev got used to it too – living with it. Lucky for him in a way. Growing up with my dad had given me a whole different outlook.

I knew with my head there was nothing wrong with being unemployed – half the country seems to be, and worse to come, Sean says (he should know, he gets the sack often enough; can't seem to settle). But something inside me made me think, if I went a month without doing something for my living I'd have more on my conscience than if I'd gone and robbed a bank.

"I got nothing to look forward to," I said to Kev.

"I have," he said. "I'm going to the Continent, aren't I."

"You are? When? You never told me!"

"I only just made my mind up."

"When are you going? Where? What you going to use for money?"

"One at a time, girl! I'm going soon as school ends. I don't know where," he said, all careless. "Probably Holland. As for money, my dad had a big win on a horse and he told me to buzz off and spend some of it."

I didn't know what to say. I was speechless really. Kev going abroad, with money of his own to spend! Just like a – well, like a man. I looked at him with new eyes. I swear he looked taller.

"Feeling jealous?"

"Yeah."

"Well, why don't *you* come?"

I gawped at him for about half a minute. Then I said, "I can't, can I. My dad'd do his nut."

He shrugged and didn't say any more for the time. But that evening he came over to my house. He didn't do that often. I think he sensed how my dad felt about him, and my big brothers – well, they *are* big: Sean's near enough six foot and heavy with it, and Vlady, though he's shorter and wears glasses, is thick-set like Dad. I think Kev was a bit nervous of them.

Anyway, this time he did come, and we sat in the front room and Mum'd got the dinner on, so she'd got no choice but to leave us alone for a bit. I heard her calling Lily and I knew she was going to tell her off to sit with us, so I quickly asked Kev, "What you come for?"

"Listen. I been talking to Darryl and them, and your pal Karen."

"She's no pal of mine, not any more."

"Well, she's Cliff's new bird. I thought if we all went together, you could come too. Your dad wouldn't kick up rough if there was a party of us, would he?"

"How could we? How could we pay for it?"

27

"Your family paid for the school trip every year till now, haven't they? Well, this could be just like another school trip. We'd only stop away about a week. We'd go on the boat from Harwich. Then when we get there we can hitch-hike. I want to get up to Amsterdam, that's where it's all going on."

"What is?"

He gave me a wink. "Dirtiest city in Europe," he said.

"What d'you mean, dirty?" As if I didn't know.

"Lot of litter and that," he said, straight-faced now. I didn't say anything.

"What do you say? Will you ask 'em?"

"How much would I need?"

He fished a piece of paper out of his pocket.

"I got it worked out. This is the fare, cheapest possible. Then you need spending money. We'd sleep in youth hostels mostly, or if the weather's good we might sleep rough."

"I'm not sleeping rough in a foreign country! I wouldn't even do it here."

"Oh, get away! That's half the fun."

I shook my head. "Not for me it's not. It's youth hostels or nothing. I wouldn't even bring a sleeping-bag."

"You can sleep in mine," he says, all sexy.

"No thanks," I said.

There was this silence. He gave me a funny look. Then he said, "Listen, Trace. I been patient with you. There's not many would have waited like I have. The lads are sending me up rotten about you."

"You said you didn't talk about me."

"Listen," he said. "Do you know what anyone else would have told 'em? At least I haven't made nothing up to stop 'em taking the Mick. I just tell 'em you're hung up on your religion, so it won't look like there's something wrong with one or other of us."

"Does there have to be something wrong?"

"Except for the Paki girls, darling," he drawled, "you're the last remaining virgin in the school just about."

"That's not true for a start."

"Your pal Karen—"

"I know about her. But there's others. I'm *not* the only one, whatever Cliff and Darryl tell you. Big talkers, small doers, them two, you take it from me." This was true. Boys aren't the only ones who talk to each other.

Kev looked amazed. "Get away," he said.

"True as I'm here."

He got this stubborn look. "Well, never mind them. It's us I'm talking about now. If we're going to Holland together I don't want to spend my time chasing you across the dykes. Are we going to have it away there, or aren't we?" And he got hold of me.

"I'm not making no promises," I gasped.

"Well in that case—"

Just then the door burst open and in came Lily. For once I wasn't sorry.

"Mum says I'm to come in and make sure you two don't get up to nothing," she says, right out, trust her. Tact! Never heard of it.

Kev was in a huff anyway so he got up without a word and marched past Lily to the front door. I stayed where I was on the sofa. I listened for the door to bang but it didn't. Lily looked into the hall.

"He's still here."

After a sec he put his head back in.

"Aren't you coming to see me out?"

That's what you call a climb-down with him, so I went into the hall, shutting the front-room door firm so Lily couldn't overhear.

"Okay," said Kev. "You win. No promises. But you will come?"

"I'll ask."

"It'll be great, you'll see. We'll have a great time." He grabbed my arm and gave me a quick one on the lips. "Start softening 'em up tonight," he said.

I brought the plan up at supper. Casual.

"Kev came to tell me he's off to Holland when school ends."

"Go on!" says Sean. None of our family's ever been abroad except Dad. "They won't let a little twit like him abroad on his tod, they'll smack his arse and send him home to his mum."

"There's a whole crowd going and all," I went on, ignoring him.

"Sure they're all mad as hatters," says Mum. "What's wrong

29

with the British Isles? If they're so keen to cross the seas, why don't they go to Ireland? There's not a bit of scenery in the world to touch the Hill of Howth."

"They're not looking for scenery, Mum," said Vlady. "Not if I know it! They want adventure."

"I wouldn't mind a bit of that myself," said Sean.

"Nor would I," I said, seeing my opportunity.

Dad put down his knife and fork and looked at me. "Ah," he said.

So then of course they all caught on, and they *all* put down their knives and forks and shouted, "AH!" like they always do when Dad does it.

Only Mum didn't get it. She was standing there with the dish of tinned peaches in her hands and she looked all round. "What's this?" She never takes in anything the first time.

"She wants to go with him," said Mary. And looked at Mum and Dad. Waiting. Were they going to let me?

"Not with him alone," I said. "With a whole bunch."

"Who?" asked Dad, short. He didn't like the idea, you could see that with one eye shut.

I told him some names, off pat. Lucky he didn't know them, except Karen. I could just imagine what he'd think of Darryl and Cliff, with their fancy haircuts and their earrings.

"I don't like that Karen," said Mum. "She's not the kind I'd want for a daughter. Not that one." She pursed her lips and doled out the fruit, splashing a bit.

Notice she hadn't said I couldn't go yet. She was waiting for Dad.

Dad ate, bent low over his dish, not looking at me. He finished in about four spoonsful and then he wiped his mouth. Nobody said a word. Then he sat back and fired a string of questions at me like a machine-gun. Who–where–how-much–how-long, where'd we sleep, what'd we do, would we stay together? I told him as much as I could and didn't get impatient or snappish. Not this time, you can bet. Then he said, "Do you really think you deserve such a thing? No O-levels. Probably not even your CSE's."

"Yes I will. One anyway." But still, he was right, it wasn't much. I should've at least tried for a couple of O's. Wished I had then, not only to put him in a good mood with me but because it was coming up for job-getting time.

"I would prefer," said Dad, slow, "that you do a job for a few months and earn some of the money yourself. That will be better."

"But Dad, then I'll miss this trip! They'll go without me!"

"There'll be other trips."

"Please, Dad! I'll work after. I'll pay you back, honest!"

"You so much want to go?"

"Yes!"

Silence all round the table. Only Vlady went on eating.

"I will think about it and let you know," said Dad. He got up and went to the door. "I don't like Kevin," he said slowly. "I wish I did, but I don't like him. I wish you had some other boy." Then he went out.

That does it, I thought. *That's a no if ever I heard one*. I felt like crying. I jumped up and was going to run out of the room, but Vlady put up his hand – he was sitting next to me – and pulled me down in my chair again.

"Don't go mad," he said.

Somehow Vlady can always calm me down if he catches me before a mood really gets started. I sat and ate my peaches and everyone talked and quarrelled and went on as usual. Lily said she'd caught me and Kev necking and I gave her a good clout for snitching. That eased my feelings a bit, but not much.

4 · Connie

I didn't sleep a wink that night hardly – well, not till near morning, anyhow. Then I slept in and was late for school of course. That meant I missed Dad, who goes off to the shop at crack of dawn.

So I had to leave without knowing what he'd decided. I asked Mum. Nothing doing. If she knew, she wasn't telling. Another bad sign. When there's good news, she tells it. Bad news she leaves to Dad.

Just as I got to the school gate I saw Kev, lurking just out of sight of the school windows. He grabbed me straight off.

"Let go, I'll be late!"

"You're late now, too late to go in. You better bunk off with me."

Tempting. But I jerked away. "I can't. If Dad found out, then it'd be thumbs down on Holland for sure."

He laughed. "Right," he said, letting go. "You be a good little girl and leave me to get on with me arrangements."

That night I waited and waited for Dad to come home. The more I waited, the more time I had to get worked up about going. At the same time I was trying to be ready to be disappointed. I was thinking, *If that cow Karen's coming, who needs it?*

But that didn't work. Because another girl from our class, called Connie Evans, told me that day that they'd invited her to come along, and she was nice. Weird, a bit, but interesting. I liked her, even though she was a prefect – the only prefect we had with enough bottle for the job. She could even keep the hard boys in order. They respected her. In a funny way, we all did.

She was a very sharp dresser. She'd dyed her hair black and she wore all black gear (not in school of course, but after). Black shirt, black trousers, even a man's black hat. She wore crazy make-ups with loads of black round her eyes, and even on her lips sometimes.

"Why all the black?" I asked her once.

You know what she said? "Black's for violence." That's all. She wouldn't explain. But I'll tell you one thing. Though she was very pretty (that's not the right word – she tried hard *not* to be pretty, but she was attractive) and all the boys had an eye on her, I'll swear *she* was a virgin – Paki or no Paki.

Anyhow, they'd asked her, probably so there'd be a girl each. And because she was brainy. She'd done O-levels, though she'd never tell how many. "She'll get our sums right for the trip," Darryl had said that morning.

Darryl was all worked up about it. He'd nearly driven me mad, talking about it every spare minute. He was borrowing his brother's camping gear, big rucksack and that. Funny, I'd never thought of Darryl as the outdoor type! Now he was rabbiting on about how the only way to see a place was to sleep in the open and talk to the "real people" in shops and that.

"How'll you talk to 'em – in Double Dutch?" Cliff asked, sneery, but Darryl didn't turn a hair.

"I dunno about double, but I'm going to learn a bit of single," he said. Cliff and me gawped at each other. Darryl learning Dutch! You'd have to have sat through four years of French with him to see the comic side of that.

I was thinking about all this while I waited for Dad to come home. Darryl being all worked up and talking about the windmills and the flowers and the canals and that lot had got me excited. Now it wasn't just a trip I fancied, it was Holland. I'd always thought it would be just flat, with the queen pedalling about on her bike, all dreary. But now I thought it might be fun, and even if it wasn't, I couldn't bear to be left behind.

So when Dad's van finally drew up I couldn't control myself. I went rushing out of the house to grab him before he'd got more than one leg out.

"Dad, can I go? Please say I can go!"

He stopped moving and just give me one of his sad, Polish looks. He didn't have to say a word. I didn't give him the chance. I just turned and ran back in the house and upstairs to my room.

Of course Mary had to be there, blow-drying her hair. It's red. She pretends to hate it, but since she found out what the boys think about red-heads she's starting messing about with it the whole bloody day practically. When I saw her now, sitting in front of our mirror blow-drying away with that silly simper on her face I just stood there and yelled:

"Why do you *always, always* have to be in here, can't you *ever* move your fat arse somewhere else?"

Red-heads are supposed to be hot-tempered but Mary's just the opposite. Not that she doesn't feel things. She just doesn't flare up like I do. She kind of smoulders deep down, like a volcano. And then, once a year, she'll erupt. . . . This wasn't one of those times though. She looked at me through the mirror and her nose went bright pink. Then she switched off the drier, laid it down ever so carefully on the glass top of the dressing-table, got up and walked out.

She brushed past me without seeming to see me. Like I was a speck of dirt. She didn't even slam the door like Lily would have, to show what she thought. She can make you feel like the incredible shrinking man, Mary can, when she goes all quiet like that. The bit at the end where he walks through the little hole in the fly-screen.

Anyway she was gone, so at least I could fling myself down on my bed and have a good cry. A good cry? What's a *good* cry? This was a lousy rotten awful stinking cry. I hate crying like I hate being sick. And at least throwing up makes you feel better after. After my "good cry" I felt just as bad as before and I looked like something the cat dragged in. Except we haven't got a cat.

I lay on the bed, thinking, of all things, *Why haven't we got a cat?* I suppose I needed something to comfort me. Something to stroke. I thought, *I wish Kev was here to give me a cuddle*, but Kev isn't really the cuddly sort. He's more sort of spiky. After this month or so we'd been going out, he hadn't got any more gentle than he was to begin with. I'd told him a few times not to grab and not to hold me so tight but he was just like that. Part of that showing-off thing; look what a hard man I am, sort of. Nice sometimes, but not when you're feeling fragile like I was then. I had a nasty feeling Kev wouldn't have been much comfort even if he had been there.

Anyway. Unless you're going to run away from home there's nothing you can do in the end but make your eyes up thick and go downstairs. When you get there you can either go on as if nothing had happened or you can sulk. No prizes for guessing which I did.

It was a king-sulk, that was. I didn't give Dad a look of course. I just took it out on everyone else. I took a swipe at Lily just for the way she stuck her elbows out when she ate. Sent Sean up rotten for losing his job again. Criticised every single bit of food Mum put on the table, though it was about like always. And told Mary to shut her face because she took Mum's side.

Only Vlady I didn't say anything to. And that was because he wasn't there. Maybe if he had been I wouldn't have let myself go. Not so bad anyhow.

"Where's Vlady?" Mum asked in a gap in my bitching. She looked round for him like she hoped he'd come and save her from my mood. It wouldn't have been the first time.

Mary said he'd gone to his evening class.

Dad smiled. He looked at Mum and she smiled back at him. Then they both went on eating and took no more notice of me. This made me feel bitchier than ever. I said Vlady's my favourite brother (or sister, if you see what I mean), but that's not to say I can always stand him being so clever and hard-working and everything Mum and Dad want, that I'm not.

"Him and his evening classes!" I said, sneery. "Big deal!"

"At least he'll have something to show at the end of them," said Mary.

"He shows off enough without another of his bits of paper," I said.

"He does not show off!" said Lily. "Not like you with your silly trips that you're not even going on!" And she stuck out her tongue at me and went *nyeeeeh*! Easy to see she'd have curled up and died of envy if Dad had said yes. The way I felt then, I'd've liked nothing better than to see her curl up and die, so I just gave her another slap.

So then she let out a squawk and Mum turned round and slapped *me*, which gave me a good reason to start shouting and carrying on as loud as I could. Dad stood it for about one minute and then he got up, picked up his plate and carried it off to eat his dinner in the front room.

"There now! You've driv' your poor father away from his own table!" said Mum. "You bad girl, you! Go away from us yourself, eat off the floor like the little wild animal you are!" And she snatched my plate and put it down on the floor in the corner.

I was beyond everything by then. I stamped on the plate and broke it.

Mum burst into tears.

I ran out into the street, leaving a trail of my dinner from my shoe across the floor to the back door.

I was shaking and crying. I didn't know how it had all happened. I was sorry. Of course I was. But I couldn't feel it yet. I just felt everything was against me. I stamped along, thinking, *Trust Dad to make an idiot of me by not letting me go! I suppose he don't trust me.* It wouldn't matter him not trusting Kev if he trusted me. I didn't need treating like a bit of fine china. I could look after myself! I wouldn't have done anything silly. Not me. I wasn't asking for trouble, anyway I didn't want them all talking about me behind my back the way they do about Karen, saying she's a slag and all that – not me! What did Dad think? I knew what he thought: he thought I was stupid, he thought a person who hadn't got a head for school had no head for living. That was his big mistake.

I found I'd walked to the tube. I stood outside, wishing I'd brought my money so I could get in a train and go somewhere. Where, though? Up West? Part of me wanted to, but another part was scared. But I had to do something. I couldn't just trail home.

I thought of going to Kev's house. It was him I wanted, more than I wanted anyone else anyhow, but I'd never been to his house – he'd never asked me – and this wasn't the time to begin. I started walking slowly, still away from home. Let's see, who else was there? Karen? You're joking! For a minute I thought of Darryl. He'd been nice that morning at school . . . but I'd never thought much of him till then. Anyhow I didn't know where he lived.

Well, what about Connie?

She lived quite near. I decided to chance it. She was a girl after all. No one could think anything about me going to see her. I turned down her street, and in a few minutes I was ringing her bell.

She answered it herself. She was all got up in her black gear. Always gave me a jump when I saw her, so different from at school, with her dyed black hair and those thick rings round her eyes. She looked a bit tense, I thought. But she smiled when she saw me.

"Hallo, Tracy! What you come for?"

"I had a row at home. I – I thought you and me might go out."

"Yeah? Good idea. Where?"

I shrugged. "I don't know, do I? Don't you know a place?" Connie's the kind of person you expect to know everything.

She didn't say anything for a bit, just stared at me. Then she said, "Yeah. I've heard of one. Never been, though."

"Where is it?"

"Down Camden Town."

"Go on – that's miles."

"Don't you want to, then?" I thought she looked disappointed, so I said, "Don't mind. Only I've got no money."

"I'll lend you."

Connie's always loaded. Her dad's in the car trade and makes a bomb. That's how she gets all her gear. She got given moon-boots for her birthday – forty-five quid, fur inside and pony-skin out. You know what she did? Sold them again – advertised them in the local paper – and bought a pair of German parachutists' boots from a surplus store. You wouldn't think there'd be German parachutists with size 5's, would you? And with what was left over – well, some of it anyway – she went down the Porto-bello and got herself all new gear, second-hand. Wet-look jeans and army battle-jackets and string vests, the lot. Dyed every-thing black that wasn't black already, and then had her hair cut and dyed again at a really good unisex place.

She didn't waste any time now. She yelled over her shoulder, "Mum! I'm going out with Tracy!" A sharp voice from the back of the house yelled back: "Yeah, you go, Connie, go quick, go on!" Somehow it gave me the shivers, that voice, it sort of cracked on the word "quick". Like she couldn't wait to get rid of her.

Connie grabbed her coat and got some money out of a handbag that was hanging over a post at the bottom of the stairs.

"Is that your mum's bag?" I whispered. The house was so quiet now her mum's voice had stopped that you had to whisper, somehow.

"Yeah. She lets me take whatever I want."

"And she lets you go out at night, just like that?"

"Course. She knows I can look after myself. Anyway it's safer out than in, some nights."

"What d'you mean?"

"Nothing, I'm joking. Come on."

That's the sort of parents to have, I couldn't help thinking.

We walked quickly to the tube, and Connie bought two returns to Camden Town.

We didn't talk much on the way. A lot of people looked at Connie. I felt dull beside her – nobody looked at me. Once I said, "Don't you mind 'em all staring?" She shrugged. "Let 'em look," she said. "They can look but they mustn't touch."

London's so big. Every tube station lets out on something different. Our station at home's like a country one, almost, but Camden Town was like another world. Not a very nice world either. Five roads led off from the place we came up at, and every one looked grottier than the last.

"Where is it, then – this place?"

"I haven't a clue. We'll have to ask."

She tried to stop passers-by, to ask the way – but you should have seen how they dodged her! They'd walk straight towards her, and then, when she tried to speak to them, they'd swerve round her in a half circle and hurry on without looking back. About four different women did that.

"Try a man," I said at last.

"Not me. I might get done for soliciting."

"What's that?"

She looked at me, surprised. "Don't you know? Stopping men on the streets to get 'em to come home with you."

"Oh," I said.

Well, I didn't know, did I? I sometimes think Vlady's right about me when he says, "It's not so much you're stupid, you're just plain ignorant. Why don't you *ask* what things mean if you don't know? You're just not interested, that's why!" But that wasn't why. I was scared people'd laugh. Even Lily laughs at me sometimes when I don't know a word. Well. At least Connie hadn't laughed.

She was trying another woman, younger this time. And this

one stopped.

"The Music Mill? Some sort of club, isn't it? I think it's up that way, on the left," she said, pointing.

We said thanks and walked on. I said to Connie, "Did you notice how they all shied away from you?"

"Yeah. So what?"

"You scare them."

"I want 'em to be scared," she said.

"Why?"

"Let 'em keep their distance."

"But then, when you need them – like just now—"

"Oh, you'll always find someone. The posh trendies'll talk to anyone. They'd talk to you if you was rolling in the gutter stoned out of your skull, waving a knife and dressed as Dracula."

We walked on through the crowd. Everyone took one look at Connie and either smirked or gave us a wide berth. When I looked at some of the types, I began to see what she meant. I wondered what sort we'd meet in this place we were going. I was a bit nervous, to be honest, but I wasn't going to let Connie see that. She didn't seem to have a nervous nerve in her whole body.

5 · The Music Mill

We came round a bend and there it was – only we didn't recognise it at first because we'd neither of us thought it'd be so big. I thought it was a bingo hall. It was a big, tall building with lots of fancy-work on the front, and a marquee like a cinema, and wide steps going up to a row of glass doors. It was lit up, and lots of kids were going in. There were all sorts, mods, skinheads, punks, and some that weren't anything interesting at all.

At the door was a big fellow. He looked us over as we came up the steps, then he stopped us.

"You girls by any chance under age?"

"Course not! Well—" said Connie. And then she boxed clever. "I'm eighteen, but she's not, not till next week."

He looked at me. "Oh go on then," he said. "I won't keep her out for a week. Don't draw attention to yourselves, that's all." And he waved us on.

The week's programme was stuck up on a poster outside. That night's group was called *Dirty Linen*. Giggling a bit, we went to the box-office and paid. £1.50 each and no readmission, so we had to enjoy it.

Inside there was a kind of lobby where lots of boys were playing the pin-tables, but we didn't stop there. Next – another lobby, this time with snooker. We could hear the music getting louder. We pushed open some swing doors and found ourselves in a kind of hall. It looked more like a cinema than a dance club. It had red walls and green floors and lots of decorations, all looking old and crumbly, with a few posters and pictures stuck around as if they'd been there years and nobody'd bothered to take them down.

There were several levels, big balconies sticking out, and little ones at the sides for just three or four people. On the ground level, there were alcoves with sofas and tables in them, and railings to lean against and to separate the people watching or eating from the dance floor. That was an area in front of the stage. On the stage was the group, playing away very loud, five of them. Only a few people were dancing so far, the rest were standing or sitting or strolling around.

Up at the very back was a bar, or two rather, one for food and one for drinks. We drifted up there first. There was a menu at the food one written in big chalk letters, with joke-things like Pink Floyd Burgers (with tomato ketchup) and Blondie Burgers (with yellow mustard) and Cool Cat Burgers (with salad). As far as I could see they were all pretty much the same, though some of them cost more.

"Can we have something?" I asked Connie. "I'll pay you back." I was half starved. After all, most of my dinner was spread out on the kitchen floor.

"Sure. Do you want a drink? We're not allowed really, that's why they got that bloke on the door."

"I only want a Coke anyhow."

We got our Coke and burgers – I had a Clash Burger; same as the others really but I was gone on the Clash then – and took them to one of the sofas and sat in a corner of it to eat. I had eyes everywhere, just taking it all in. The music was too loud for talking. There were loads more people coming in every minute.

"How long does it go on for?" I yelled at Connie.

"I don't know. Till late."

"How'll we ever get home?"

"Oh, get away, Tracy! We only just got here. Enjoy yourself."

I wanted to – I really did. But how? I mean, it was fun just being here and seeing it, but to really enjoy it you've got to take part. Taking part meant dancing and for dancing you need a boy.

Not that there weren't plenty about. All shapes, sizes and colours. Some nice-looking ones, and all.

"What you think of the caryatids?" Connie asked me suddenly.

I looked at the group, bashing away – two electric guitars, a sax, trumpet and set of traps – funny mix in a way; lots of beat and noise but nothing special. Good enough for dancing though, if only someone'd ask me. "They're not bad," I said. "I like less beat and more tune myself."

She looked at me, and right off I got that prickly feeling you get when you've made a tata of yourself. "Hang about," I said,

41

"aren't they called *Dirty Linen*?"

Connie pointed. "The caryatids are them," she said.

I looked. She was pointing at some big men's figures, statues, very muscly and with curly beards, holding up the little balconies on the side walls. I hadn't even noticed them till then. I felt a proper idiot, but at least she hadn't laughed or said, "Fancy not knowing that!"

"This was a theatre once," she said, "or maybe a music hall. Nice one too, by the looks of it. Bit run down now – seen better days. Pity. Still, at least they haven't pulled it right down and built something horrible instead."

I sat there not talking. I liked Connie. I was grateful she'd brought me to this place when I was miserable. But I'd suddenly remembered all those O-levels. It set her apart from me somehow.

I hardly noticed when this boy sat down next to me on the sofa until he started chatting me up in a break in the music.

"Haven't seen you two here before."

"We've never been here before, maybe that's why."

"Great, eh?"

"It's all right," I said, trying not to sound bowled over.

"What's your name? Mine's Gary Sharp."

"Tracy Just." I pronounced it like the English word, not "Joost" which is a short form of Dad's Polish name. We all use that because no one can pronounce the long form.

"And who's your friend?"

I kind of introduced them. He kept staring at Connie. He wore old-fashioned flared jeans and a black wet-look jacket with lots of stickers on it. Not what you'd call a raver, but he wasn't bad. He chatted me up for a few minutes and offered to buy us Cokes. I opened my mouth to say yes but Connie nudged me.

"That's all right thanks," she said. "We just had one."

The band started up again and this Gary hesitated. Something told me he wanted to ask Connie to dance, but in the end he asked me. He led the way down the stairs and onto the dance floor and we did some pogo. I don't like trying to talk while I dance (how can you?) but he kept sort of shouting questions at me through the throb and the blare. Finally I stopped dancing and said, "I can't hear a word you're saying. Can't we just dance?" That shut him up till the break. Then as we walked back up the stairway he said, sarky, "Can I talk *now*?"

"*Now* I can hear you," I said.

"Is your friend a real punk? Or is it just a front?"

I stopped dead and looked at him. I'd never thought of it like that.

"I dunno. You better ask her yourself," I said — and then could've bitten out my tongue. Because of course that's just what he wanted to do. And for the next hour he sat between us on the sofa with his back turned to me, talking to Connie.

I got fed up with this finally and wandered away. I wished I had some money. I was still dead hungry and I didn't like to ask Connie for more. For once I wished I smoked. If you're on your own and feeling awkward at least it gives you something to do with your hands. A guy near me saw me looking at his fag and offered me one, but he looked a bit of a creep so I said, "No thanks." I don't really like the taste anyway.

"Oh go on — you know you want one. You won't drop dead from your first puff, you know, whatever the government health warnings say."

I was bored. That was the trouble. You'll do anything to stop being bored. I took one and he lit it. I puffed on it, trying not to inhale. Just the same I got tears from trying not to cough. This boy was watching me.

"Call that smoking?" he said. "You'll never get the big C. like that you know! Take a real drag." He showed me. As if I'd never seen anyone smoking before! Karen's been at it since she was about twelve. And Kev smoked every day, on his way to and from school. He was getting a real addict. His breath smelt sometimes, though I didn't like to mention that. He might have got hurt and stopped necking.

"It's no good," I said. I looked round for somewhere to put it out.

"Just drop it on the floor," he said. I looked at my feet. The carpet, or whatever it was, was littered with ends. I tried to drop it but it was like the spray-can on the bridge. My hand kind of wouldn't open. I was seeing our carpet at home. Sean dropped a butt on it once. Just once.

"— Or, here — give it to me. Pity to waste it." And he took it and pinched it out with his fingers. Then he put it back in the packet. "Want to dance?"

And how. But I didn't know about with him. Funny thing, attraction. He wasn't any worse-looking than Gary, but somehow he didn't turn me on. He had a real flat brush-cut on top and long hair at the back, and an earring, and a T-shirt with *I'm for Two-Tone* written on it. I looked at his face quickly to find just something I could like. Well. His nose was all right. But is a nose enough?

Still, he had legs and arms. He wasn't asking me to marry him.

"I don't mind."

"Come on then." We started off down the steps and he stopped. "Want a drink first?"

I was going to say no, but he was already making for the bar. He came back a bit later with two glasses of beer.

"I'm sorry, I don't like beer," I said. I thought, *That does it, he won't dance with me now, he'll think I'm a right nutter.*

But he didn't mind. "All the more for me," he said, and, opening his mouth, poured down first one half-pint and then, while I stared, the other. I'd seen them doing it on telly once, but never in real life. "So what would you like instead? A short?"

You can't go on saying no all the time.

"I'll have a gin and orange," I said, casual. Never had one before in my life of course. *God,* I thought. *What if that bloke on the door could see me now?*

He was back in a flash with this drink in a small glass. "Get it down you and let's dance," he said.

I got it down me. Not bad. My eyes watered a bit.

"Come on then, girl," he said. He grabbed my hand and next thing I knew, we were dancing.

He was a good dancer. I think. Or maybe it was the gin. That gin and the two I had later. They'd've made a good dancer out of a one-legged kangaroo. I won't say I was stoned. Just floating about, kind of. All the lights spinning around twice as fast as we were. I think I fell over once, or almost. He caught hold of me and set me up again like a skittle. Gave me a little push, and I started pogoing again.

And that was another thing. The music. I never liked it very loud. Hurt my ears, made me nervy. Now, sound doesn't come louder than in the Music Mill. They've got amplifiers there would make your average disco sound like a budgie chirping in the next room. But I didn't mind. I liked it. I even loved it. Usually I feel like the noise is trying to do a break-and-enter job on my skull. Now, thanks to the gin(s), I felt that it was already in there, somehow. No use fighting it. Just had to let myself go with it.

Once or twice I saw Connie, dancing with Gary. She waved to me. After a while I stopped seeing her.

When we weren't dancing we sat in one of the boxes the caryatids were holding up. It was great up there, like being up in the clouds, looking down on a mad world. This boy naturally wanted something back for all those gins and that, but when I didn't want to, he didn't push it. We talked a bit. He seemed to live for the Music Mill; no job, slept all day and came to the Mill at night. Knew all the groups. He was some kind of squatter he said; he wasn't from London. I could've told that from his accent. I'm good on voices. He was from Manchester.

After a time – a long time – I had to go to the toilet. It wasn't very nice in there and I didn't hang about, but when I came out I couldn't spot him. He'd gone from the box and I couldn't see him anywhere about, though I walked all round the hall looking. Not that I specially wanted him, for himself; he'd just got to be a sort of habit. Anyway he'd gone.

Someone else was in our box, so I went and leaned against the railing above the dance floor. I wished Kev was with me. I still felt a bit floaty from the gins. I watched the dancing while the music throbbed in my head like the time I had flu so bad I got delirious. I got ever such a funny idea while I stood there, watching all the jumping and jigging going on below. I thought if those caryatids just bent forward a bit, the boxes on their heads would get thrown down onto the dancers, like in *The Phantom of the Opera* when the chandelier falls down and crushes the people underneath. . . . Then I had another funny idea. The music was so loud, you might not have heard the crashes and screams, not if you hadn't been watching. . . . I looked round at the caryatids. They looked like big white devils. I gave a shiver and turned away.

I think the gin was wearing off. Maybe that's why I started

45

thinking of home and what Mum and Dad would be doing and what they'd say when I got back. I said before I don't think ahead much. I just let things happen. But once I get started, I can't stop.

It must be getting late. . . .

What was I thinking about, coming here in the first place? It wasn't even a Friday or Saturday – I'd got school tomorrow! I must be crazy, hanging about this club or whatever it was – I wasn't even enjoying myself any more. Dad'd have my head on a plate the minute I got in the door.

Suddenly I got all panicky. I wanted to leave, now, right away. I looked round wildly for Connie. Had she gone off without me? Would she do that? Karen would, like a shot, if there was a boy in the picture. I didn't know about Connie.

I ran down the stairs to the dance-floor. They'd dimmed the lights till you couldn't see anything clearly, they just had these spotlights on the band. . . . I looked for ages, straining my eyes, but I couldn't see her. What if she'd really gone? She had all the money and – I remembered with a nasty shock – my return tube ticket. What'd I do if I couldn't find her?

I went out into the lobby, cursing her under my breath, telling her what I thought of her. And there she was, playing snooker with Gary.

Well, I pinned a grin on and went up to her.

"Con, I think we ought to go."

Of course I thought she'd stall a bit, now she'd found a boy. Who wouldn't? I might myself. But she didn't. She looked at her watch and said, "God, you're right! It's after one o'clock!"

Panic? I hadn't known what it meant till she said that.

"*One o'clock?*" I almost shrieked. "You got to be joking!"

She showed me the watch. There it was in red glowing figures, *01.10*. I wished I could crawl under that snooker table and die.

"How'll we get home? Con! How'll we get home?"

She didn't seem fussed at all. She laid down the cue and turned to Gary.

"You got a car?"

He shook his head.

She smiled at him. "Not to worry, we'll manage. Come on, Tracy."

She just walked off. Gary ran after her, through into the next lobby where all the pinball gambling machines were flashing like mad.

"Here, hang about! I don't know where you live!"

Without stopping she threw back at him, cool as you please, "You don't have to."

"But I want to!"

"I'll be around. Anyway I'm only sixteen. I'm not meant to be in here really."

That stopped him short, but only for a minute. As we went out the swing-doors into the open, he came rushing after us.

"No readmission!" Connie sang out, just before he let go the door. He stopped again and stood there, staring after us as we walked away into the dark.

"Didn't you like him?" I asked, although I was in such a state by now I didn't really care.

"Yes, he's okay. Nice talker. Not grabby."

"So why did you run off like that?" She was striding along fast, with me having to run to keep up with her.

"He was good enough company for an evening but he's nothing special."

This seemed to me a bit funny. Unnatural. I mean, for a girl who wasn't going with someone already . . . you'd think she'd want him to phone her. But I couldn't bother about that now. It was after one o'clock in the morning. *Mother of God!* I thought, *What'll I do?* And that was praying, not swearing.

"What'll we do, Con?"

"Well, I know what I'm going to do," she said, still cool. "I'm going to sleep in King's Cross station, and go home on the first tube in the morning."

I nearly dropped.

"Sleep in a station? All night? What'll your dad say?"

"Nothing. I done it before. He don't mind."

"I don't believe you!"

She shrugged. "Don't then."

I suddenly started to cry. It just came over me. Connie came back to where I was stuck in the street there, blubbing.

"What's up?" she asked, quite kindly really.

"Maybe your dad won't mind, but mine'll bloody well murder

me!"

She gave me her hanky and said, "Okay. Blow your nose while I think." She stood there looking into the road. There was still a lot of cars going past. I guessed what she was thinking.

"And I'm not thumbing a lift neither, so don't suggest that! This time of night, anything could happen!"

She put her arm round my shoulder. "Look, Tracy," she said, "you know what you better do. Call your dad. If he's like you say, he'll be waiting up. Dead worried most like. Ask him to come and get you."

My first thought was, *I couldn't!* But my second was, *What else can I do?* Maybe he'd be relieved to hear from me, maybe they'd been so worried they'd forgiven me for what happened at supper. . . . Even if not, what could I do? I wasn't staying out all night in some station; I didn't dare.

I swallowed. "Okay. Give me 5p for the phone."

I found a phone box and dialled our number. Dad answered after the first half-ring.

"Tracy?"

"Yeah, it's me."

"Where are you?"

"At Camden Town station."

"Are you alone there?"

"No, I'm with Connie."

"Stay still. Don't speak with nobody. I am coming now."

Connie stayed with me till Dad came, but she wouldn't come back with us. As the car drove up and I said, "Here he is!" she just gave my arm a friendly squeeze and said, "Good luck. I'm off," and walked quickly away. I called her, but she didn't turn. Weird. Maybe she liked sleeping in the station.

I didn't have time to wonder about it because Dad had thrown open the door of the car and there was nothing for it but to get in.

We drove as far as the beginning of Westway before he said one word. I looked at his profile. All the ballooniness of his nose and lips was drawn together in lumpy ridges from his scowl. I was trembling. He'd never hit me. Well, once he did – just once, when I'd really scared him with my temper. But his words could sting worse than slaps. Now, even his silence hurt. So much that in the end I said:

"We didn't do anything bad. Just went to a sort of disco hall. It's not a bad place."

Dead silence.

"I was just so fed up. You don't know how much I wanted to go on that trip."

"When you are too old to have such tempers," he said. "When you are more mature. Then you can travel. Travel is a wonderful thing. One must not take it for granted. In Poland the government keeps the people's passports. They cannot go abroad to see other countries unless the government allows. If we lived in Poland, you would realise that foreign travel is a privilege. Too good to waste on silly bad-tempered children."

What could I say. Incredible-shrinking-man time again. I just curled up in my seat and stared out of the window. I was shivering.

Dad glanced at me. "You're cold," he said accusingly. "Why you go out at night without your jacket? Is stupid." He turned the heater on. "Your mother has been crying all evening," he said. "Herself she blames. What did she do to blame herself for? Why should she cry? I'm asking you."

I knew that that was one of those questions that doesn't expect an answer, but I answered it. "She put my supper on the floor," I said. "I'm not a dog."

"You acted worse than a dog," he said. "For being a mother and punishing you for your nastiness, she must blame herself? Let the ones who don't care, blame themselves. Let the ones who don't punish, blame themselves."

I thought of Connie's parents. "Dad, what would you have done if I'd stopped out all night?" I asked.

He gave me a look then. "You are sixteen," he said. "If you were fourteen, or fifteen, and you stay out all night, perhaps I take my belt off. But you are sixteen. You are nearly a woman. You stay out all night, that means you think you are grown up and can do what you like. You don't accept my authority. I have no way to control you. You are too old to beat, not old enough to leave home. To say the true, I don't know what I would do. It is hard to be a father. Don't make it harder."

I'd thought I was in his hands, but think how I felt when he turned round and put himself in mine! What could I do except say, "Well, I thought of it – but then I decided not to." I didn't add that I'd been dead scared of the idea of spending the night sitting up in King's Cross station.

Dad said, "Good. I sent your mother to bed. In the morning, I want you should apologise to her. Will you do that?"

"Yeah."

He didn't say anything else till we got home. He parked the car and we sat for a moment in the darkness after he turned off the headlamps.

"Dad."

"What?"

"Thanks for coming."

"Don't thank me for that, Tracy. I was glad you had sense to phone and ask. I would always come. I told you."

"Dad—"

"What now?"

"Is there no way – no way at all – that you would change your mind about the trip?"

"You choose a bad moment to ask me."

"Is there, though?"

After a long pause, he sighed. "Tracy. I don't like your friends. I'm sorry."

"Is that the main thing?"

"It is one thing."

It didn't seem to be a thing I could do anything about. I just crept upstairs. I was shivering all over. Mary was fast asleep of course. My bed was turned down. I threw off my clothes and crawled in, expecting the icy sheets. The most lovely heat spread all over me. I couldn't believe it, but it was true. Mum had taken her electric blanket, that Dad gave her for Christmas, off their bed and put it in mine. Now why would she do that? Had she done it out of love, or just to make me feel lousy, after I'd made her cry the whole night? If she had, it worked. But not for long because I fell asleep.

6 · Michael

No prizes for guessing how I felt about getting up for school, what seemed like two hours later. I even had a hangover. I suppose that's what it was. Headache and that. Mouth all horrible. Never again. (That was all I knew!)

Mum pulled me up somehow. She didn't say a word about last night. I remembered I promised Dad though, so I said, before I'd had time to think about not wanting to, "Sorry." She sort of went "Hmp". Then she said, "Put on a clean blouse. Wash your neck first." *Wash my neck!* I ask you! As if I was ten years old. Of course I got the message. I'd *acted* ten years old. Okay. Fair enough. I shut my mouth and washed my neck. Mary was still asleep. Her job in Woolies doesn't start till nine-thirty so she doesn't move till nine. I was glad. Fewer questions, the better.

Lily was wide awake though. Isn't she always?

"Where did you go bouncing off to last night?"

There was only her and me at breakfast. Sean was helping in the shop while he was looking for a new job. Vlady of course has a steady job with British Oxygen ("Bock" we call it.) They give him time off to go on studying. He hadn't gone to work yet, but he eats early and then studies in his room. I was glad he wasn't there to ask questions. As it was just Lily and me (Mum was out hanging washing) I was able to give her a good answer.

"I went out dancing. And drinking. And smoking. And I picked up a boy – two in fact. And I came home at two a.m. And I've got a hangover. So now you know." I went on eating my sugar-puffs.

She just gaped at me. Of course she thought I was making it up.

"Liar!" she said. But she wasn't quite sure. I didn't say another word.

For once I was dying to get to school. I wanted to see Connie. Would she turn up? Well, she did, and looking none the worse for her night in the station. She was her school-self again, all nice and clean, blazer and flat heels like the rest of us, eyes looking smaller without the black, hair brushed down instead of up. She's like two people. I think that's how she wants to be.

"How was it?" I asked.

She shrugged.

"No, honest – tell me. Where'd you sleep?"

"On a bench."

"Do they let you?"

"They don't stop you. Lots of people do it. People waiting for early trains and that."

"But what if someone came up and started with you? I've heard there's gangs, just on the lookout for young girls—"

"There's always a couple of coppers there to keep an eye on things. Nobody tries it on with me anyway. Not when I'm in my gear, they don't."

"What time d'you get home?"

"About five-thirty, six. Time to have a bath and change and have something to eat."

"And your mum and dad didn't say a word?"

"Mum asked where I'd been. Dad was asleep. He don't get up early."

"She doesn't mind?" It seemed crazy to me, not like a real mother.

"I told you. She trusts me."

I thought of what Dad had said – "I wouldn't know what to do." Some kids I heard of left home altogether, they just bunked off and never came back. Maybe Connie's parents were just glad she didn't do that.

"Maybe they think, if they get mad, you'll leave home for good," I said.

"I would, too," she said.

"How could you? What would you live on?"

She smiled. She had this very sweet, innocent face, round and rosy, like a baby's, but there was something about her mouth – a little bit crooked when she smiled.

"It's not hard to live away from home," she said. "Lots of kids do it. You get in on a squat somewhere. You work when you got to. Some of 'em con a bit, or go on the rob, but I wouldn't do that, that's not my style. I don't mind work. Just not for too long

52

at one thing, that's all. There's Social Security, too, if things get too tough. Oh, you won't starve if you leave home."

"You sound as if you're planning to."

"I've thought about it. There's nothing to keep me at home."

"Don't you – you know – like your parents?"

She lifted one shoulder again, that way she has. She was keeping something back, I could see.

We were standing in the playground. Suddenly up rushed Darryl.

"Hi!" he yelled. "Hallo, girls!" He was all lit up, even more than yesterday. "Guess what? I've got a job after school! Butcher's boy, me! Saturdays all day and all. By the time we leave for Holland I'll have earned enough to buy myself a two-man tent!"

"I thought you was borrowing your brother's?"

"That old thing! It's dropping to bits. No, I seen one at the sports centre. Nylon, light as a feather, built-in ground-sheet, fly-netting, extra rain-cover, aluminium poles that fold up short. . . . Special offer! My dad's giving me a little portable stove for my birthday and all. Listen, you two got to be nice to me from now on, and whoever's the nicest, gets to share my two-man tent!"

"Are we really the men for the job?" says Connie. "Oh well, after all, Holland is the land of *dykes*!" And she let out a shout of laughter at her own joke. (I only got it after I asked Vlady. All right. I'm naïve. Can I help it? It's my upbringing.)

Connie sloped off then, which left Darryl and me walking in to class together. Everyone hooted and someone yelled out: "Oooh! Where's Kev?" But Kev was nowhere in sight.

"Where *is* Kev?" I asked. "Bunked off again, has he?"

"Suppose so," said Darryl. "Listen. You coming to Holland then?"

I shook my head. His face fell. But he just said, "Well, that's too bad. Would've been nice, the six of us."

Cliff and Karen were sitting in the back, heads together. They'd got a map of Holland spread out on the desk. Karen looked up at me.

"Coming with?" she asked. First time she'd spoken to me since the row we had.

53

"No I'm not, so what," I said. *God* it hurt when I had to say it to her.

"Why not?"

"My dad won't let me," I mumbled. I felt like adding, "because he don't like my friends, for example you."

"My dad wouldn't let me either," she said, "at first. But I kicked up so rough he backed down. I said I'd leave home."

Another one!

"Why don't *you* try that on?" she asked me.

"I don't want to, that's why," I said back, sharp.

She shrugged and went back to Cliff and the map. Cliff went on looking up at me for a moment. He gave me this kind of sympathetic look. *Huh*, I thought. *Some best friend, that Karen. She don't care as much as these two boys who I never even spoke to much, till we started planning this bloody trip I'm not going on.*

Those last days at school! I tell you, I almost felt sorry for the teachers. They'd've had to set fire to themselves to keep us looking at them. Most of the boys were lying about on the desk-tops, or sitting with their backs to the front chatting up their mates behind them, or reading comics, or throwing stuff. One of them even lit a fag and sat there puffing it till the teacher, who was fed to the back teeth with the lot of us, came up the aisle and swiped it out of his mouth.

The same thing was in all our minds – X more days and we're free! We'd learned all we were going to, this time round anyhow. Outside the windows it was summer . . . how could we listen? Some of the teachers didn't even try, they let us play games or have silent reading periods. Nothing very silent about them, nor much reading neither. Still.

That day finished, finally. We sloped out of school. I felt all limp and fed up. What was going to happen to me? If only I had the trip to look forward to, before I had to start thinking seriously about a job. I kept thinking of Mary, lying in bed till the last minute, then dragging herself off to work. Every day she'd come home looking fagged out. If you asked her, "How was it?" she'd curl her lip up and say something like, "Great. I love it. So exciting. So stimulating. I think I'll go to hell instead. Be more lively anyway." Mum'd tut at her and she'd say, "Honest, Mum, wailing and gnashing of teeth'd be more interesting than the noise of my cash-register." Mum'd say, "But it's better than some jobs, surely? Than a factory? At least you're seeing lots of different people all day." But Mary'd say, "Mum, they're not different. After a bit they're all exactly the same. And they're all horrible."

Got me scared, Mary talking like that. I always knew I'd never face a factory job. But if shop assistant was no good either, what was left? An office, Dad said. For that I'd need typing. At least. Maybe shorthand as well. You get good money for that straight off. But I didn't fancy it, somehow. . . . Maybe I could work with Dad, in his shop. As a boss, Dad'd have the advantage of not being sexist (or sexy, come to that). But Sean grumbled every day about lugging the cartons, stamping on the prices, the fussy customers, the *boredom*. Of course, Sean loves to moan, always did. Still. He didn't make it sound the job to keep you happy for life, exactly.

While I was walking slowly along thinking about all this, I found myself crossing what I privately called "Bastard Bridge". I looked sideways at my paintwork. At first when I saw it by daylight it gave me a nasty feeling. First, feeling guilty because of Kev, and second, feeling guilty about doing it at all, even if I'd written he was an angel. But somehow, now I'd stopped worrying about the message. I couldn't resist just glancing at it and thinking, *I wrote that.* Everybody saw it, and noticed it. So far no council workers or anyone had come to take it off so perhaps it'd be there for ever – till after I was dead, even. What chiefly bothered me now was that the writing was so bad, and that, even in that little bit, I'd managed to make a spelling mistake. I'd looked up "bastard" in the dictionary. . . .

Suddenly I saw Kev. He was sitting on the low wall on the corner of our road. I saw him before he saw me. He was leaning against a brick post having a smoke. He *was* good-looking – handsome, even. And he was mine, my boyfriend. What if he was a bit rough sometimes? He wasn't a bastard! No, not Kev! Suddenly I wished the council men would come, I wished they'd come tomorrow, and clean off what I wrote.

I ran the rest of the way to him.

"Oh," he said, "there you are. At last. I been waiting hours.

Can I come to your house tonight?"

"If you like. But what for?"

"I heard your dad said no. I got a plan. To get him to change his mind."

"Some hopes!"

"You might get a surprise."

I did and all.

I told Dad he was coming, but of course I didn't say why. Dad always likes to put a clean shirt on if someone's coming to the house, no matter who it is. Nothing he hates more than being caught out in the shirt he's worn all day. Even though he wears an overall at the shop. He's ever so clean, my dad is.

When the doorbell rang I let Lily answer it so Kev would come in and see me in the front room reading a magazine and looking casual. Don't ask me why. Mary does that so I do it. "Never seem too eager," she always says. Why not? Don't they like it better if you're pleased to see them and run to the door? But Mary's my model when it comes to men. She knows it all by instinct.

So the door opened and in came Kev all right, but he wasn't alone. I jumped up, feeling all awkward and nervous in front of a stranger.

"Trace, meet Michael. He's Darryl's brother."

Well, I could see that, now I looked. He was a lot like him, only his hair was longer and he was taller and more developed. He had Darryl's snub nose and nice-looking face, without the spots too. He had freckles instead, and darker hair. Not much of a trendy dresser, but the jeans and polo neck suited him.

"Hallo, Tracy," he said and we shook hands. Then we both looked at Kev.

"Your dad home?"

"Yeah, he's through in the kitchen."

"Can we have a word?"

"What you up to?"

"Never you mind. I told you to leave it all to me."

I led them to the kitchen. Mum was washing dishes with Lily. Sean and Dad were at the table reading the papers. Well, Dad was reading. Sean was looking at the evening's programmes.

"Dad. Kev wants to see you."

Dad stood up. Kev introduced Michael. Then they all sat down at the table.

"Mr Just, I brought Michael round because he's coming to Holland with us. You see," he went on, so polite I could hardly believe it, "Darryl, that's my mate from our class, his parents is like you and Mrs Just, they didn't want to let Darryl go off by himself, I mean just with other kids his age. But they said, if Michael would go with us, like to keep an eye on us, see we take proper care and don't get into no trouble and that, well then they wouldn't object. And what we was wondering was, whether that might make a difference to you too."

Mum'd turned round from the sink by now and was staring at Michael. Dad too.

"How old are you, son?" he asked him.

"Nearly nineteen."

I knew what was coming next.

"You have a job of some kind?"

Dad judges everyone in the world by whether they work and how hard and what at. I held my breath and prayed. *Please let him be in work and let it be the kind of work Dad approves of!* Because with him, just any old job won't do. It's got to be something that he counts as "constructive". He'd rather him a gardener, for instance, than, say, selling swag in Southall Market or working for a bookie, or flogging magazine subscriptions, even if he was making a bomb at it.

"I'm a builder's mate," he said.

I looked at Dad, quick. It was exactly what he likes – making things. From his little smile I could see it was well on the right side of whatever line he draws in his mind between what's useful, and "being a parasite", as he calls a lot of jobs.

"You are a regular builder? You put up good buildings, for people to live in and work in?"

"Well, I'm renovating old ones at present, but my firm does all sorts."

"That's nice," said Dad. "It is good to build."

I breathed again. It was all right. That part, anyway. But that wasn't the end of it. It'd take more than an honest job to change Dad's mind about Holland – I knew that.

"When you go to Holland, will you take with you a girlfriend?"

Trick question! But that was all right too, because Michael said, "No. I haven't got one."

Sean looked up for the first time. He's nineteen too. He hasn't got a girlfriend either. For all his noise and rude jokes at home, he's too shy. He's like a great shambling idiot around girls. He gave Michael a look of interest and went back to his TV programmes.

Dad was asking another question.

"When you get to Holland, why you won't want to go off by yourself? Why you won't be bored to be with a crowd of young kids?"

I thought to myself, *If this is all a put-up job, if they're making it up about him coming, that'll do him*. But what did he say, quick as anything? "Well, Mum's helping pay for my trip on condition I stop with them. I never been abroad. I want to go. That's part of the deal. Anyway my brother Darryl's okay. He's not a baby. We get on fine together. I'll like teaching him camping and that. It won't be boring, how could it?"

"You have met the others? That Karen—?"

Michael shrugged. "Yeah. Karen. Look, Mr Just. I can't be responsible for all of 'em all the time. If they want to be silly I can't stop 'em. But if they want to be sensible and see the country and that, I'll do my best for 'em." He gave me a quick look. "Your daughter don't look like a silly girl to me," he said.

Dad smiled, reached his arm out and put it round my waist. "Well," he said, "appearances can mislead. But I hope you are right. Time will tell." And there was a silence.

The three of us – Kev, Michael and me – all looked at each other. Mum looked at Dad, and I saw Dad give a little movement, half-shrug, half-nod. And suddenly I felt something like a rocket zoom up inside me and explode in my head.

"Dad!" I nearly yelled. "I can go!"

Kev broke out into a great soppy grin. Mum sighed and went back to washing-up. Lily looked like the sky just fell in on her. And I did a little dance round the room and then hugged Dad so hard he nearly fell over, chair and all.

7 · Ready for the Off

When you look back on something big, like a trip, you can make a pattern out of it – a picture, kind of, in your mind. It has its own colours. If it's all yellow and shiny, you're lucky. The shine can dazzle out any black patches where things went wrong, like spotlights shining in your eyes. But if there's too many black bits (and specially if they come near the end) they got a way of growing. Afterwards, when you're remembering, you forget the nice bright parts were ever there. If you're not careful, that can make the whole thing seem as if it wasn't worth doing.

So what I want to do is remember the good bits because there were plenty, really – as well as telling about what went wrong.

Things started great. There we were, a gang of us, starting off on a great adventure together. We'd been like that ever since school finished and we really started getting ourselves ready to leave.

Michael did the bookings and that, and each of us had to get the things on our lists. The lists we made together, at a meeting we had. Michael told us most of what we ought to get. You should have heard the yells and groans as that list got longer and longer.

"But what do we need tents for? I thought we was going to sleep in youth hostels!"

"Plates – cups – frying pans – I'm not going to do no cooking! Don't they have take-aways in Holland?"

"Sleeping-bags – where'll I get a sleeping-bag for cripes' sakes?"

Michael wouldn't be shaken on any of the stuff he thought we should have, nor on the way he thought we ought to do everything. But it was when Karen asked, "How we going to carry all this clobber?" that Michael really sprung his big surprise.

"On our backs. And on our bikes."

"BIKES!"

Michael looked round, cool as you like, at us all with our

mouths wide open.

"Yeah, bikes," he said. "Hadn't you lot realised this was going to be a biking holiday?"

Well, then there really was a proper outcry. We could all ride bikes, and most of us had one – of sorts – or could borrow one off somebody. It wasn't that. It was the idea that we were going to have to pedal-push our way all over bloody Holland when we'd thought – well, I don't know what we had thought, come to that. I think I'd thought of myself riding about in other people's comfortable cars.

But as Michael talked, it began to seem stupid, the idea of hitch-hiking. No car can take on seven at once, we'd have had to split up right away. And the whole idea was to keep together. Michael explained the roads were flat and that most of them had cycle-tracks beside them and that loads of people cycle everywhere in Holland. "Anyhow," he said, "that's what we're doing. We put our bikes on the boat at Harwich, take 'em off at the Hook, tie on our stuff and off we go. I got a campers' map of the country. We'll buy nosh in the markets, eat by the roadside, stop wherever we like to look at things and explore or swim or anything you like. It'll be great, you'll see, you won't know yourselves."

"He sounds just like a scoutmaster or something," muttered Karen.

"Yeah," said Kev, not muttering. "You're not taking a bunch of snotty-nosed kids on a day-trip you know. I'm not keen on all this health-and-strength lark. I'm not the athletic type, me! I want to get up to Amsterdam and do the town over with Tracy."

"Well, Amsterdam's a good sixty miles from the Hook," said Michael. "That's a lot of distance, however you do it. The Dutch don't like giving lifts, especially to little English lads with comic hair-cuts. You might spend half your holiday standing on a roadside with your thumb in the air if you're not careful. Why don't you stick with us? We'll go to Rotterdam instead. There's a terrific tower there, taller than the Post Office tower, you can go up it and see for miles. And we're going to Madurodam."

"What's that then?"

"It's a whole miniature town. No, don't laugh. I've seen pictures of it. Honest, you never saw anything like it. Must be one of the wonders of the world."

There was a hoot from the boys. "He thinks we're bloody *kids*. Honest to God! He does! Dolly houses—"

Michael looked put out, and I thought, *He'll leave us to get on with it in a minute*. But suddenly Connie, who hadn't said a word till then, just sat there painting her nails (black), piped up.

"I saw a miniature village once. It was great. And I fancy seeing Rotterdam. My grandad seen it right after the Germans bombed it flat in the war."

We all looked at her. She held up her black nails to admire them. You never saw anybody look less the roughing-it type.

"What do you think about camping and biking and that, though, Con?"

"It sounds okay, why not? Long as we don't have to knock ourselves out. After all, it's not le Tour de France, is it?"

"No," said Kev. "It's le Tiptour through le Tulips."

We all gave a howl. But after that there wasn't too much argument, somehow. We all just let Michael have his own way.

*

I'm going to skip over the preparations. There was panic-stations a couple of times, about equipment and that, but Michael seemed to have a lot of connections – mates he'd been camping with who lent him stuff to fill the holes in our lists, and in the end most of our families came up with bits of cash for extras. Vlady put his racer into good nick and lent it to me (along with two hours of instructions) and bought me saddle-bag things to hang on each side of the back wheels. Sean dug out his old rucksack that he'd got on special offer years ago and never even used, and gave me that as a present. He gave me some instructions too – in fact the whole family had a go at me.

Sean said, "I don't see why you should be getting abroad before I do, but if you must go, watch out for these foreigners. They'll do you up any way they can. Keep your money and passport and that in a bag round your neck. In Italy they snatch it off you in broad daylight if you got it in your hand."

"I'm not going to Italy, though, am I?" I threw back at him. I wasn't ready to believe anything bad could happen, and because of that I threw back most of the warnings I got from the family.

Mum's was, "The dear knows why you'd want to go to Holland of all places. You'll hardly find a good Catholic there in a day's hard march; Protestants to a man, so they've no morals, of course. Be on your guard against the men, don't let anyone in your tent at night. . . . Oh, Jesus, Mary and Joseph, why do you have to be going off at all? I think your father's lost his senses altogether!"

Mary said, privately in our room, "Never mind the Dutchmen, Tracy, you watch out for Kevin. I know his type, let him out of sight of home and he's up to any old tricks. Just you keep yourself to yourself and don't let him talk you into anything."

I didn't like that, of course, and I told her pretty sharp she didn't know him and should keep her tongue off him. It worried me, secretly, because Mary has this instinct about men, like I said before – I've never known her wrong unless she's been daft over one herself. But I got over it by sulking with her for a day or so and then forgetting what she'd said.

Vlady talked to me while he showed me all about his precious bike and how to take care of it (I didn't even take a day to forget all that, of course). He said we should be careful to make a good impression in Holland, that people who travel abroad are like representatives of their own country and that the foreigners judge your whole nation by what you do. There was nothing in that to get my back up so I paid more attention to Vlady than to any of the others; like I always do, really, because I love him best.

I don't include Dad in that, of course. Dad's lecture was the longest and the most boring because it was all the others rolled into one and went on over the whole two weeks before we left. I took in anything that didn't seem to criticise Kev, and ignored the rest.

We got off at last. In the end all the family helped, even Lily (*her* "lecture" had just been about being sure to bring her back a present). The girls helped me to pack my rucksack and saddle-bags and Sean showed me how to keep my new sleeping-bag rolled up in its little canvas sack-thing, Mum made sure I had all my money and tickets and passport safe. At the last minute Dad gave me an extra fiver and such a tight hug I was breathless before I started.

We got the train to Harwich from Liverpool Street, and from

that straight on to the boat. It was a Dutch boat, so we could feel right off we were in a bit of Holland – if only by the prices. Everything was double, even a cup of tea.

Of course, the boys had another use for their money – the one-armed bandits. Karen too. Connie said she wasn't throwing her money away, and that helped me not to – I won't say I wasn't tempted, especially when Kev was winning. But in the end he was down two quid. He didn't tell Michael (who was on deck at the time) and he said he'd do me in if I did. If you ask me, he was a bit scared of Michael, even though he kept saying he wasn't taking orders from *him,* and that he'd best not start being too bossy.

It was a night crossing and we all slept in sort of lean-back chairs – quite comfy except your neck got stiff and it was hard not to let your mouth fall open. Not that we slept much. Truth was, I felt a bit funny about sleeping with all those boys around me. Specially when Kev reached over and tried to touch me up in the night. I did wonder how we'd arrange the tents and all that. We'd only brought four – the girls didn't have to carry tents. Who'd share with who? We hadn't talked about that.

Still, it sort of added to the excitement. When Michael woke us up and there we were, in Holland, *Abroad*, I think everyone felt the way I did – that we'd never be quite the same after the week to come. How right we were!

8 · Bikes and Dykes

Right from the off, I took to Holland. I don't know why. The port was nothing to speak of, and even when we got out of the town (which was hairy, cycle-track or no cycle-track!) there was nothing much to see.

But, like Michael said as he stood by his bike, breathing deep and looking all round at the flat countryside: "Cor! What an eye-stretcher!" And it was. My eyes were so stretched they almost popped out – after London, where they're brought up short every two yards, they hardly knew how to focus so far.

The others weren't committing themselves, except Con, who breathed deep as well and said, "Smells different, anyway." It did, too, and after the coffee factory in Acton, that could only be an improvement, though it was mainly just the sea, so far, that we were smelling.

Me, I felt all worked up and full of go. I looked along the flat, straight road reaching into the distance, and jumped astride my loaded bike like a cowboy jumping on his horse.

"Well, let's go if we're going!" I yelled, and took off. When I looked back, they were all streaming along behind me.

Mile after mile! Michael soon overtook me on his newish racer, but he didn't go too fast. We had time to look round. Not that there was much to see, not at first. But I'm funny. I've always liked being around water. Never mind what kind, sea, lakes, rivers, anything (even a nice bath'll do if nothing bigger offers!). And here was enough water for anybody. It was more than half water, some of the way. Great shining sheets of it, with roads and fields in between, and these big dykes, like high grassy banks, running for miles with roads along the top so you could ride up there and get a good view.

I rode alongside Connie.

"What do you think so far?" I asked her.

"Ain't half a lot of sky," she said.

In London you don't look up much. It's either sunny or it's

grey. But here, spinning along these dyke-tops, the sky seemed to be three-quarters of the world. Blue, with every sort of cloud in it, little wispy ones and big bunchy ones and that sort that's like the sand, far down the beach at low tide, wrinkled and ridged. The sea was a bright line, far away.

I rode faster and caught Michael up.

"What's this place called?" I asked. I knew he'd brought a guide-book and knew a good bit to begin with. He'd kept telling us we ought to read up on Holland before we came, only we hadn't of course, only maybe Darryl.

"I think we're in Zeeland," he said. "Sea-land. It used to *be* sea. All this water's bits of the sea that they haven't pushed back yet. The land part's called polders."

We were riding along one of the dykes. On the sea side the water lapped the foot of it, like a huge reservoir. On the other side were neat little houses and fields and orchards and stuff.

"If this dyke wasn't here—"

"—all that, there, would be flooded. Yeah."

"Let's stop. I want to look."

Michael put up his hand and we all stopped. There was no other traffic. The road wasn't even a proper smooth road, it was made of bricks. There wasn't a soul in sight except an old farmer digging his vegies below us on the land-side. I kept running from one side of the dyke to the other, thinking what would happen if the water got higher or the dyke broke.

Cliff and Kev and Karen were standing on the sea-side, looking down at the water at the foot of the bank. Michael had his back to them, pumping up his tyres. They started fooling around. Cliff gave Karen a push, and she grabbed him and screamed. Gave me a fright in the middle of all that quiet. Con, too. Con shouted, "Oh shut up!"

"Who are you telling to shut up?" asked Kev, turning round and coming at her. "You're not a bloody prefect now, you know!" He got hold of her and started dragging her along. It was all for laughs of course, but she pulled back and Kev yelled, "Here, Cliff, let's get her!" The pair of them chased her along the edge of the dyke and then they caught her and made like they were going to shove her over – there was no fence or anything, just a grass slope straight into the water.

65

Karen, Darryl and me stood watching. Uneasy somehow. I'd done plenty of scuffling and shoving in the school yard, but here it was different. I felt I ought to go and help Con but I didn't want to get involved. I looked at Michael. He was crouched by his bike, looking over his shoulder. Frowning, but not getting up.

"Knock it off now," he said, but they didn't even hear him. Con was really struggling now, with the two of them pushing and pulling her towards the edge. And suddenly she lost her temper.

I haven't mentioned Con's temper. When she was a prefect she usually kept very calm, but just sometimes, when some kid would cheek her or ignore her, she'd do her nut. There was one black sixth former who kept pushing past her when she was on dinner-duty and swearing at her and that, and finally she lost her rag and clouted his head. What a fuss! He yelled and raved that she was picking on him because he was black, and she got suspended from being prefect for three weeks. Only she was the best they had, so they had to reinstate her in one week. I'll tell you, that was one week of chaos at dinner-times.

Now she lost her rag again. She pulled loose and gave Kev one shove. I let out a scream then, because over he went, straight down the bank, arse over tip.

Michael was up on his feet like a shot and half-way down the bank, sliding and grabbing the grass to keep from falling. Kev tried to stop himself but he couldn't. Hit the water with a walloping great splash. That stopped him!

There he was, half in, half out, holding on to great handfuls of grass, yelling what-for up at Connie, who was leaning over with a face like chalk. Michael slid down and grabbed him by the scruff and yanked him onto dry land.

"You bloody nutter!" he said. First time I'd seen him lose his cool.

"She done it – she pushed me over!" Kev yelled. He looked ready to cry, he was so cold and wet, and the fall and everything. I felt sorry for him, even though he'd started it. As he came scrambling up to the road again I wanted to run and put my arms round him. I more or less did.

"You okay?"

"Yeah. But I'll get that rotten cow," he said, glaring at Con.

Well, Michael made him change his gear. He tied his wet jeans to the back of his rucksack somehow so they flapped about a bit as we rode in the hopes of drying. Horrible things, wet jeans. Kev was still in a rage; he wouldn't talk to Con. I rode alongside him now. Michael didn't say anything else but you could see what he thought. His lip was sort of curling. I thought to myself, *I hope he never looks at me like that*. I hate being made to feel small. It's something my brother Vlady's very good at.

After a bit we came to a little town. After that we were so busy looking round we forgot what happened before. You had to cross a bridge to get to it – it was like on an island – and there were great twisted towers by a gate like a castle gate in a fairy story.

Inside the town it was all a bit like that too: cobbled streets, the houses and the town hall and that all old, some of them leaning a bit, but all ever so nicely kept up. The town hall had a fantastic clock tower with a little metal man who clonked the bell every hour, with a statue of Neptune on the very top. Everything dead clean, the streets and that.

We were walking along, just strolling, looking in the shops, and Cliff got out a packet of fags and lit up. He gave one to Kev and that was his last, so naturally he chucked the packet away, like he would at home. Michael was walking ahead with Darryl and didn't see this happen, but somebody else did – two of the locals.

It wasn't some little old lady, neither, it was a young couple, walking towards us. They stopped dead in their tracks when they saw that fag-box hurtling into their nice pure gutter. Boggling at it.

"I hope it's not going to be like this everywhere," Kev muttered. "We'll never have any fun if they're all so bloody uptight. Bet you when we get to Amsterdam we'll see lots of decent gear, and discos and that. That's where it's all at, is Amsterdam."

"But Michael says we're not going to Amsterdam, it's too far."

"I'm going to Amsterdam and I don't care what Michael says," said Kev. "And you're coming with me."

"How'll we get there?"

"On a train of course," he said.

I didn't know what to say, so I didn't say anything.

We had a sort of picnic meal on the grass outside the walls of the town. It was ever so nice there by the water. Michael didn't exactly tell us not to leave litter, but when we were packing up I saw him quietly picking up a few bits and pieces and putting them in his pocket.

"How much further we going today?" Cliff asked. The boys had a lot of clobber, really a lot, and they weren't used to biking with all that on their backs.

"The camping site's another fifteen miles," said Michael.

"Fifteen miles!" Heavy groaning all round. "Why can't we stop here? There must be a youth hostel!"

"We ought to leave youth hostelling for the towns," said Michael. "It's good weather for camping. Silly to lug those tents and then not use 'em. Come on, we'll be there before you know it."

We set off again. More nice flat roads. Lovely not to have traffic to speak of, and even at that there were these cycle tracks so you never got scared some speed-merchant was going to zoom by and land you in the ditch. London seemed as far away as the moon.

I was thinking of something – something I was trying to remember. About dykes. Something I read once, when I still read kids' books. I shouted across to Kev:

"Here, did you ever hear about a little boy who put his finger in a leak in a dyke?"

"Blimey, get a leak in one of these things and you couldn't plug it with an elephant's bum!"

*

We got to the camping site around tea-time. It was pretty full, but not too bad. We found a good place for our tents and started putting them up while Michael settled up with the owners or whoever takes the money. By the time he found us, all hell'd broken loose.

This time Michael just stood there with his hands on his hips, roaring with laughter.

"Easy to see you lot don't know one end of a tent from another!"

Darryl was the only one who'd got his tent to stand up at all, and even his sagged in the middle like a wash-line when the pole's blown down. Cliff was inside his, crawling about like a cat in a bag, struggling with the aluminium bits and yelling to Karen to pull on ropes she couldn't even find. Kev and me were holding his up from each end, standing there sort of helpless – you'd think we'd got a tiger by the tail and whiskers between us and didn't know what to do next.

"One at a time," said Michael. "Come on, I'll show you."

So he gave us a demonstration, and we soon got the idea. While I was sticking Kev's skewers into the ground I started worrying again about the sleeping arrangements. When the tents were all up (more or less) I dragged Connie off to the toilet (the Dutch even manage to be clean about *that*).

"Where you going to sleep?" I asked her.

I was always afraid Connie was going to jeer at me; I don't know why because she never did. This time she just said, "With you, unless you got other plans."

"Oh," I said. "No."

When we got back to the others they were all crawling in and out of each other's tents and joking and fooling about. Kev came up to me straight off. "Come into my parlour said the spider to the fly."

I crawled in on hands and knees. There wasn't much light in there, but enough to see what he'd been up to. Our sleeping-bags – his and mine – were lying there side by side. All cosy.

"Oh, no!" I said. "OH no you don't!" And I started heaving mine out again, sharpish.

I should have known better. In a second I was flat on my face on top of the sleeping-bag, and he was flat on his face on top of me.

"Gerroff!" I shouted, pushing at him. We were rolling about, with the built-in ground sheet crackling underneath us.

"Sshhh!" He put his hand over my mouth and tried to reach round and kiss me, but I ducked.

"GERROFF!" I yelled again as soon as I got my mouth free. I started wriggling out backwards. I got my feet out of the slit in the tent and started kicking like mad. The whole tent must've been heaving about. I felt my foot hit the front pole.

"Will you stop it? You'll wreck my tent!" said Kev.

"So let me out!"

Just then I felt someone take hold of my ankles and pull. Out I slid backwards with Kev riding on me like whatsisname and Flipper.

Kev jumped up quick then, of course. His face was beet-red. He stalked off. Karen and Con, who'd pulled me out, were laughing their heads off.

"What was he up to, Tracy? He can't have been very good at it, from the sound of you!"

"Listen," said Michael. "Don't yell the place down. You're disturbing people. Now then, who's for a cuppa?"

He was good at that, I'd noticed – calming us down without getting mad at us. We all brought our mugs round his little camping-stove where he'd got a kettle boiling and he made us tea with tea-bags and milk from a carton. Tasted great. There were biscuits too. Dutch ones that he'd bought us in that town. I could've eaten the whole packet. Kev came mooching back after a bit. Nobody said anything. I gave him a grin to show no hard feelings. I just wished he'd get his timing right. Or maybe it was as well he didn't. That tent had felt ever so private and cosy. I wondered what it'd be like at night. . . .

When we'd sorted ourselves out we walked around the site, chatting people up a bit and finding out the score from the ones that hadn't only just come. Michael palled-up with a couple of the grown-up lads and was making notes about places to go and things to see.

"D'you like Michael?" Con asked me.

"He's all right. It's good he's with us. We'd be pretty useless on our own."

"I'm not so sure I like him leading the way all the time."

"Would you know where to go and that, by yourself?"

"Where to go? I'd go where I liked, what's to stop me?"

"But you might get lost – ride for miles – I mean if you didn't know where the camping places were."

"Listen. I got my sleeping-bag. I got my knife and fork, and a change of gear, and some money. How many barns did we pass today, even in the loneliest spots? Haven't you ever dossed down in a pile of hay?"

I stared at her. "No. And neither have you."

"All right, I haven't, but I wouldn't mind. Then in the morning you could go to the farmer and get a drink of milk and some fresh bread—"

"Get away, how would you ask?"

"Like this," she said, and she pretended to milk a cow and then drink, and then slice bread and eat it. "And if they didn't get that. . . . Well, maybe I'd take Darryl with me. He knows the Dutch for milk and bread."

I never know when she's serious. Would she really do a bunk and take Darryl? I didn't believe it, but with her you never know.

When we'd finished wandering about it was seven o'clock. The three boys'd crawled into their tents for a kip – one boy, one tent. Karen was off somewhere. Michael was sitting outside his tent reading his guide-book. Con and me went and sat next to him.

"Where we going tomorrow?" I asked.

He showed me a fold-out map and pointed. "We'll head for Rotterdam."

"Kev wants to go to Amsterdam."

Michael shrugged. "Can't stop him. He'll be knackered if he tries it by bike."

"He says we'll take a train." I slipped the "we" in kind of mumbly, but he heard.

"*You*'re not going, are you?"

Now I shrugged, not looking at him. He didn't talk for a bit, but finally he said, "I told your dad I'd look out for you. I can't if you take off."

"She can if she likes," said Con.

"Of course she *can*," said Michael. "She's not paralysed."

I changed the subject because I didn't know myself if I wanted to or not. "What we going to do tonight?"

"I thought, a campfire. I got us some Dutch sausages and lager."

That perked us up. Took both our minds off leaving the group.

Trouble with campfires in Zeeland is, there's not enough wood. Still, we found the odd crate and that, and a place where it looked like there'd been a fire before, and as soon as twilight came we lit it.

Right away every other camper in the place rushed towards us, and soon you'd have thought you were at a boy scouts' jam-

71

boree. People from all over the place were sitting round our bit of a fire – Germany, France, Belgium, you name it. The "camp commandant" as they called him came belting over to complain, but Michael took him aside and next thing you know he was sitting down with us sucking beer from a can and even joining in the sing-song that some of the Dutch kids started up.

They're dead organised, those Dutch. Two of them went round collecting up what everybody had to eat and giving it out again so in the end we got bits and bites of food from all over the blooming continent – all kinds of sausages (none as good as Dad's Polish ones, but some weren't bad), buns and rolls and sweet biscuits and some of that Swiss chocolate, and sauerkraut. And loads of different kinds of cheese. We threw in some of our Mars bars which the Dutch boy carefully cut up so everyone got about one crumb – honest, talk about the loaves and fishes!

Somehow we all filled up. Then the drinks went round. Beer, lager, fizzy drinks, and some wine. I never tasted wine before – didn't like it much. The Dutch boys nearly finished us off when we were all calling out our national toasts. Like, the French said, "*Bon santé!*" and we said, "Cheers!" But then when it was the Dutch kids' turn, they all shouted something that sounded like "*UP YOUR GAZOONTHITE!*" They couldn't understand what we were laughing about.

Even after all that, those Dutch kids hadn't had enough of organising us. Next thing was, all the groups from the different countries had to sing a song or do something to entertain the rest. Right off, guitars came out and an accordion. My heart sank a bit. What could any of *us* do? Not one of us played the guitar. As for singing. . . . Well, I suppose we could sing a bit like anyone else, but not good enough for a public performance. Me, I'd have died sooner.

While two French boys were doing a fantastic clown's act, good enough for *New Faces* any day, Michael was looking round at all of us, his eyebrows asking, "Can anybody fly the flag for Britain?" The boys pretended not to notice. Karen and me put our heads down on our knees. Con didn't say anything.

I leant over to her. "Can you sing or something?" I whispered.

"Course I can sing, who can't?" she said.

"You better then, 'cause none of us can."

She looked straight at Michael and said, "I will if you will."

He looked back at her. He smiled into her eyes. First time I noticed what a sweet smile he'd got, like Robert Redford's. "Okay," he said. "You first. Mine goes on all night."

So when the Dutch boys shouted across the fire, like TV announcers, "Now it is the turn of Great Britain!" we all boosted Con onto her feet. Everyone clapped and cheered her on. When Michael smiled at her, I'd wished I was in her shoes. Now I'd rather have sunk through the ground. The firelight shone on her face and about thirty pairs of eyes were glued to her, and there came this silence, waiting. But she didn't care. She didn't even giggle or anything. She just opened her mouth and sang.

She still had her way-out look, even in her cycling gear. Instead of blue jeans she'd got baggy Annie-Hall trousers – black of course – with her wet-look jacket over them, loads of badges and that, and she'd dyed her hair fresh just before she came and even bleached a stripe down the middle of it. So naturally she had to sing a punk song, even though it sounded a bit thin with no backing.

> *We don't want to make the grade.*
> *When you make the grade you feel afraid.*
> *And you look back down at your pals below.*
> *And you just don't want to know.*
>
> *We don't want to make it to the top.*
> *When you get to the top you got to stop.*
> *And when you stop at the very top*
> *You stamp on the hands below.*

I didn't like it much. And I thought Con didn't either. She was singing it to fit her image, but it didn't fit the place or the mood. So when they clapped her she said, "Now I'll sing a different kind." And she stood still (she'd been shaking around before, real Bette Midler stuff) and sang an old Beatles number off a reissue. I only vaguely knew it, but there was a Belgian there with a guitar and he started to back her. All the songs and acts so far had been loud or funny or punk, and then came Con's second

73

song, and it was a real contrast.

The words were so bloody sad! That poor old priest that nobody ever came to his church except when they were buried. . . . I was crying almost. And what a voice! We never knew she could sing like that. We were all giving each other looks. Darryl's mouth hung open, staring up at her.

When she finished she just sat down again, cool as you like. There was a pause, then everyone started clapping and cheering, and I wished I was her again, or just me with some talent.

Then it was Michael's turn.

You couldn't say *he* wasn't nervous – he was. When it came to it he tried to cop out, but everyone sort of got under him and shoved him on to his legs. He said, "I hope most of you speak English because I'm going to say a long poem." They all gave a cheer and he took a deep breath, and was off.

Long! I'm telling you! It must've been about fifteen verses. It was the one about the little boy called Peter that stuck his finger in the leak in the dyke. Only it turned out to be his whole hand. It was still pretty far fetched and it didn't half go on, but somehow it was good. The bit I liked best was when this Peter first heard the trickle of water coming through the leak. Later – much later – I got Michael to write that verse down for me.

> *But hark! through the noise of waters*
> *Comes a low, clear, trickling sound;*
> *And the child's face pales with terror,*
> *And his blossoms drop to the ground.*
> *He is up the bank in a moment,*
> *And, stealing through the sand,*
> *He sees a stream not yet so large*
> *As his slender, childish hand.*
> *'Tis a leak in the dyke! He is but a boy,*
> *Unused to fearful scenes,*
> *But young as he is, he has learned to know*
> *The fearful thing that means.*
> *A leak in the dyke! The stoutest heart*
> *Grows faint that cry to hear,*
> *And the bravest man in all the land*
> *Turns white with mortal fear.*

> *For he knows the smallest leak may grow*
>   *To flood in a single night;*
> *And he knows the strength of the cruel sea*
>   *When loosed in its angry might.*

Well. Maybe it's a load of rubbish. I don't know anything about poetry. But I like it. I liked the way Michael said it and the way they all listened. And they all clapped their heads off at the end, so I wasn't the only one.

9 · Darryl

There was a good bit of mucking about, about the tents, before we all settled down. Because if you work it out, seven people into four tents won't go, I mean not if three of the people are girls.

In the end it was me and Connie in one, Kev and Cliff in one, Michael and Darryl in one – and poor old Karen all on her lonesome in the other. At least, she was all on her lonesome to begin with. Her tent was next to ours and there was a good bit of giggling and scrunching around in the middle of the night, but Con didn't say anything and neither did I. It wasn't Kev I could hear whispering and scuffling in there and that was all I was worried about.

Packing up next morning was a dead bore. Rolling the tents up tight enough to squeeze back into the tiny little duffle-bag things took hours and we got fed up and narky. Michael was ever so patient, showing us what he called short-cuts to doing things, and managing to organise us without us minding. Karen actually cooked the breakfast. It was only hot hard-boiled eggs but she did it. You'd have thought it was a four-course meal the way she went on about it. She never cooks at home. Her mum won't let her, she's so cack-handed.

We set off latish, but it didn't matter. We'd just begun to realise time didn't mean a thing to us any more. No more alarm clocks to wake us up for school, nobody telling us to get a move on or we'd be late . . . no more horrible buzzers to make us change classes, or bangs on the bathroom door, or a big sister telling us it was her turn for the mirror. And nobody nagging us to do chores or homework, or yelling that the dinner was going cold. We were on our own.

While we were riding along, I said to Connie, "Isn't it great, doing what we want when we want?" and she said, "Yeah, it's like old Shaughnessy was always going on about, natural rhythms." Miss Shaughnessy was our science teacher. It was great to feel our natural rhythms could bang on without her in future!

Michael led the way to a little market. Kev and Cliff bought cans of Coke and as near as they could get to what they ate at home, but I was getting in the mood "to go Dutch". I watched what Darryl and Michael bought. They were standing by a push-cart that had a barrel on it. Out of this the man took little silver fishes, all dripping water. Someone would buy one and put their head back and gobble it down like a sword swallower and then pull out the skeleton. Michael did it too, but he spat most of it out. Darryl watched carefully and when it was his turn, he did just the same as the locals and afterwards swore it was delicious.

Me, I went for the fried fillets they served from another stall. No batter on them, it was just strips, but it tasted great – fresh, like the sea smells. I could've eaten ten of them. I made do with five.

Kev came up to me, munching little thin chips.

"What's that rubbish you're eating?"

"It's good. Give us a chip."

He gave me one, putting it straight in my mouth. Then he looked round a bit to see none of the others was near enough to hear, and said, "Let's do a bunk."

"When?" I asked.

"We're heading for Rotterdam, ain't we? Bet they got trains there for Amsterdam all the time. We could just give Michael the slip in the traffic."

I wasn't keen. I suppose he saw my eyes stray to Michael.

"You fancy him or something?" he asked me, sharp.

"Course not!" The idea gave me a jump, somehow. "Why?"

"You're always looking at him."

"I am not!"

He put his arm round me. "I don't want to spend another night like last night," he said. "Didn't sleep a wink. At least not till Cliff got out." He looked at me straight. "You know he had it off with Karen last night."

"So *he* says," I said.

"He did. But then anyone can make it with Karen. I'm glad you're not like her."

I didn't say anything. I was remembering the noises coming from the next tent in the night. Cliff had made it all right, and

77

then gone running off first thing to blab to Kev. It made me sick, to be honest. I mean I'm no prude, at least I try not to be, but if *that* isn't private, what is? I couldn't help wondering what would have happened if it'd been *me* in a tent on my own.

Of course if it'd been in the middle of a field somewhere, with no others near it, that would've been different. Or would it? I wasn't sure how I'd have felt, to say the true.

"Listen," I said. "Why can't we stick with the others? It's fun so far."

"Speak for yourself," said Kev. "It's not my idea of fun. I can do without all this fresh-air-and-exercise kick. Me back aches and me lungs is gasping for a breath of petrol fumes. And what's the opposite of claustrophobia? 'Cause I got it. All this space is giving me the habdabs."

"Well, but we're going to Rotterdam, that'll be shut-in enough for you . . . ."

"I'll tell you where I want to be shut in. In a two-man tent with you."

"Can't put up a tent in a town, stupid. And youth hostels is segregated."

He gave me his last chip and lowered his voice a bit more.

"Listen," he said. "Darryl ain't the only one who's been working. You know when I bunked off school those days? I was doing some odd jobs. Picked up a bit of the needful, more than a bit if you want to know. So you and me, we don't have to depend on youth hostels, or tents. We could go to a hotel."

Would you believe it? A hotel! Just like that!

"Well, what do you say?"

"You're crazy," I said. But he must've seen a bit of me liked the idea (and don't ask which bit).

"I'm crazy about you," he said.

He'd never said anything like that before. Never looked at me like that before either. We just stood there staring into each other's eyes. I felt woozy. His eyes were blue with little brown bits like chocolate flakes. He'd filled out a bit lately. His shoulders too. I won't say I didn't fancy him because I did. I let myself think about being alone with him in a hotel room, all nice and private and clean, with our own bathroom and the sheets ironed. . . . Turned me on a lot more than thinking about rolling

78

around in a tent, I can tell you. Matter of fact it turned me on a bit too much for comfort. I moved away from him.

"Where you going?"

"Back to the others."

"Cop-out!"

"Okay!"

"So you won't come?" he asked, following me close, panting down my neck like a bloodhound.

"I never said that. We'll see."

"Oh all right, play hard to get then! Maybe I'll take Connie instead."

Honest, boys are so babyish. So *obvious*. It's hard to keep respecting them. Even Lily wouldn't pull a silly trick like that to get her own way. In that moment I swung right away from the idea, right away from him.

"Ask her then, and see how far you get," I snapped, and ran off to where we'd left our bikes.

*

I rode the next hour or so with Darryl.

It was funny about Darryl. I'd known him six years and never paid him a bit of notice. He was just a dumbo who sat in the back of the class and hadn't even sense enough to resent the Irish jokes, which could easily all have been about him. That was what I thought.

But there's some people who're not dumb really, they're just kind of asleep. Give them the right sort of prod, and they jump up and start sending off sparks in all directions, like a catharine wheel.

Ever since the off about this trip, he'd been like a different person. Running all over the place, working, talking, learning even. I'd laughed at the idea of him learning Dutch in a couple of weeks when he hadn't learned to say *Bonjour Madame* in six years. But he'd done it. Oh, not properly, of course not. But he had his phrase book he'd bought down the High Street, and he'd learned to say good morning and how do you do, and how much is this, and which way to the gents and quite a lot more besides. Now when we were shopping for food, or eating in a café, he insisted on ordering in his terrible Dutch, and he didn't care if they didn't understand a word and he had to point it out in the phrase book. He just kept on at it. He was the only one of us that bothered to figure out the guilders and that, too – the rest of us just held out some money and hoped they'd be honest and take the right amount.

As we rode along you could see Darryl thought the world of his brother, he kept bringing his name into the talk.

"Wasn't Michael something else last night? That poem?"

"Yeah, it was all right."

"He half brought me up, you know. Specially since Dad went."

"Went? Where'd he go?"

"Died, didn't he. Three years ago."

"Oh." Mum always says "passed away". "Went" could mean anything.

"He's the eldest, see. There's five of us. Mum couldn't manage on her own."

I wondered if my mum could have managed if Dad had died. I bet she could. Lots of widows do. So without thinking, I asked, "Why couldn't your mum manage?"

He didn't answer for a minute. I could hear all our tyres swishing along the track. Just before he did answer, I suddenly remembered.

"She gets ill a lot."

Boozed, more like. There'd been talk at school. Still, I liked him for covering up for her.

"He's clever, you know. Wanted to stop on at school, take A-levels. Only once Dad went, he had to leave and get a job. On the building three years now. He'd like to design 'em, not build 'em, and he could, too, if he'd had a chance, if Dad hadn't gone."

I was thinking about Kev, though, and what Con had said. I interrupted him. "Darryl, if Con was to ask you to do a bunk for a bit, just her and you – would you go?"

He looked at me, surprised. He had this rough, reddish hair, curly now it was beginning to grow out of its punk cut. He had freckles. I hate freckles, I could never kiss a boy with freckly lips. You can't see where they finish, they're all sort of smudgy. Still, you don't have to fancy a boy to like him. I liked Darryl better than Cliff, even if he was a bit wet sometimes. Darryl only acts hard.

80

Now he said, "Con don't fancy me, she thinks I'm thick."

The minute he said that, I knew he liked her. It just figured, a kid like Darryl fancying someone sure of herself, like Con.

"She said you'd be useful, speaking Dutch and that."

He swerved a bit and then straightened up his front wheel.

"You mean, she's actually said something about it?"

"You know Con. She doesn't like to be with a crowd. She's a loner."

"The cat who walks by himself."

"Eh?"

"It's a story. *I am the Cat who walks by himself.*" He was staring straight ahead across his handlebars now. "I always thought I'd like to be like that. I can't be, though. I can't stand being alone for five minutes."

Me neither. Well – ten minutes maybe, when I'm miserable. *The cat who walks by himself.* Yeah, that was Con all right, specially in her black get-up, and her dyed stiff hair brushed up on end like fur.

"Would you go though?"

He shook his head, still looking ahead. "I wouldn't like to leave Michael," he said. "Anyway she probably didn't mean it. She wouldn't take me. Never."

No opinion of himself, that's his trouble. And stuck on Con. Poor old Darryl.

10 · Dutch Disco

We didn't make it to Rotterdam that second day. We found a nice camping spot and spent the night there. Funny how easy it was to put the tents up the second time. We weren't so tired either. Just as hungry though. This site had its own canteen, sort of, where you could get snacks and even hot meals. We all had the same – sausage and chips. Well, frankfurters, really. The only really Dutch thing was that you could have apple sauce with them. Naturally only Michael and Darryl did. I nicked a bit of Darryl's just to try. Not bad by itself, but you can't tell me it goes with chips.

Karen came up to me just as we were eating.

"Can I sleep in your tent tonight?" she whispered. "Connie won't mind sleeping on her own, will she?"

"What's wrong?" I asked her.

She went red in the face a bit, and looked away. "I've gone right off Cliff after last night," she said.

So that's what she was sulking about all day – not leg ache at all. I thought it was the other way round, the boy doesn't want the girl any more after. I didn't know what to say. I was off Karen. But there she was, giving me this begging look, and we had been friends a long time. Once. So I said, "I don't mind if Con doesn't. Only what's Cliff going to say?"

"I don't give a *shit* what he says!" she said, half shouting suddenly. I wanted to put my arm round her then, only you can't, can you. Everyone thinks you're a Les.

I had to fix it with Con. She just gave a shrug and said, "Don't blame her. He'd better not come slithering in on top of me, that's all!"

"Don't you like him?" I asked.

"No. Either he's a fool or he's NF. I've always wondered. You know when he first had his ear pierced, he came to school with a gold swastika hanging off it. I told him to take it off. He wouldn't, so I grassed to Barry." Barry was our old form teacher.

"*He* had it off him in five minutes. He was in the war and all, when he was young, same as my grandad. *He* can't stand nothing to do with the Nazis."

"My dad lost all his family in the Polish concentration camps."

Con looked at me. "I never knew that," she said.

We didn't have a camp-fire that night because we heard there was a disco in the little town nearby and we all went to that. It was a proper riot. The Dutch really let their hair down. I danced with a couple of Dutch boys. One looked very Dutch, blond with blue eyes and this big, pale face like a lump of dough, but very sweet somehow, though he couldn't talk English. We just smiled at each other.

Later on we went outside for him to have a fag, only turned out it wasn't a fag he wanted, it was a quick grope. Nothing doing. So we sat on a bench and he smoked with one hand and held mine with the other. I let him do that because we had to do something instead of talking.

Suddenly someone grabbed my free hand and pulled me onto my feet. Kev, of course.

"I been looking for you!" he said, furious. "What you doing out here, as if I couldn't guess?"

"Listen, I was just—"

"You come inside with me," he said. "And you—" he shouted at the Dutch boy—"you can piss off!"

Well, it seems this lad could understand a bit of English after all, because his face turned brick red in the light of the lamp we were sitting under. The doughy look wasn't there any more; he looked like a big angry hard man. He got slowly to his feet and Kev suddenly saw he was six foot tall and with fists like cauliflowers. He shrank back. Well, who can wonder? He'd be a fool not to.

"Cripes," he said under his breath. "Come on, girl, out of it!" And he pulled me back into the disco-hut. We started dancing and soon worked our way into the middle of the crowd. Kev'd got the white face now.

"What you mucking around with him for?" he yelled at me through the din.

I wouldn't answer. I reckoned till we'd been to that hotel it was none of his business who I mucked around with. I wasn't, anyway.

"You nearly got me in dead trouble!"

"You nearly got yourself in, you mean."

"You was holding his hand; I saw you."

"I had to do something. We couldn't talk."

"Maybe *I'd* better forget English then!"

We danced till near closing time, all except Cliff. Poor old Cliff! Karen wouldn't dance with him, and nor would Con, and somehow he didn't have the bottle to tackle the Dutch girls. I had to dance with him myself in the end, he looked so down, just hanging around smoking.

Kev was off in the toilet round the back, so I just went up to Cliff and said, "Want to dance?"

"Don't mind," he said, but he chucked his fag away sharp enough.

The reason I haven't described Cliff is because it's hard to. He's not got any definite features really. He's the kind you wouldn't notice in a crowd, even if it was a crowd of five people.

I remember one time at school, he was walking home with four other boys, including Kev and Darryl, and he smashed a Pepsi bottle in the gutter. A man was just getting into his car. He heard the crash and called them back. Of course they just ran like rabbits, shouting rude things back over their shoulders. So this man chased them, in this car. They ducked up a one-way street and he lost them, but he complained to the school. Said he'd got a good look at them and could identify them.

Well. So he could. All the other four. But Cliff got away with it, just by being like he is – dead ordinary. Thin, pale, neither tall nor short, with this mousy hair. Maybe, I thought to myself as we danced, that's why he wears swastikas and makes National Frontish remarks to shock people. To make himself noticed. He would choose a girl like Karen, too. Anybody choosier wouldn't have looked at him. Unless she felt sorry for him, of course, like I was. Not that sorry, though. His hands are damp and he smells funny. Not bad, just funny.

Kev came back from the bog, but he didn't do his nut this time. He just waited till I was done dancing with Cliff and then he came up to me and said, "It's late. What do you say we start walking back?"

"Yeah, why not? Only let's tell Michael where we are."

"What's it his business?" Kev said. But he let me sort Michael out and tell him we were going. He was dancing with this Dutch girl. Ever so pretty she was. Lots of curly hair. And she was wearing this kind of rose-coloured skirt. We were all in jeans of course, and they were getting pretty grotty-looking too. I looked at her white blouse and thought, *I'll wash all my stuff before I go to bed tonight, even if I do have to carry it wet tomorrow*. Not that I'd brought anything like that, all frills.

Michael said we might as well wait because it was nearly over and we could go together. But Kev was signalling me across the room and I said, "We'll just go ahead." He looked at me a minute, then gave a bit of a shrug and went on dancing.

Kev and me started walking along the narrow streets of the town. It was dead quiet. We strolled along, between the dark buildings with their funny high pointed roofs. There was a moon. It was ever so romantic. I just wanted to walk like that, quiet, hand in hand, and not talk or even think much, just drink it in. But Kev's not the quiet type.

"What sort of a dancer's Cliff then?"

"Okay."

"They say if you dance well together, you're good in bed together."

So that's how his mind was working. No surprise, I suppose, a night like that. I got a sort of thrill up my back myself. So I said, nice as I could, "He didn't dance that well, not with me."

"You and me dance well." And he put his arm round me.

I looked back along the old-fashioned, empty street. No sign of the others. Kev edged me into a doorway. Long pause in story-line.

"Listen," I got in at last, "it's no good for tonight, if that's what you're hoping. I'm dossing with Karen, and that's it."

"Please, Trace. Don't be like that." He was nibbling me all over my face and neck now, and suddenly he put his hands where they shouldn't go. One hand, anyway – the other was round my waist. First time. I've seen it so often on telly I thought I knew what to expect, but honest, when he touched me there I thought my knees'd give way. I couldn't breathe right. I just stood there with my eyes shut, not thinking, not moving, just feeling. It was so exciting, I forgot where I was and everything. I even forgot who was doing it to me.

I didn't go for that. So I kind of made myself come to, and moved his hand. Not pushed it, mind you. Just moved it nicely.

"What's wrong with you?" he asked, quite loud. Jarring.

"Nothing. Not a thing," I said, trying to make my voice come out normal, but it didn't. "Only let's – keep walking."

He dropped me like a hot potato. "Oh well then – that's all, folks!" he said, very loud now, and he sang the loony-tune like at the end of the cartoons. And he stuck his hands in his pockets and marched off, leaving me to trail along behind.

I ran after him. I didn't want to be left alone. "Don't be hurt, Kev," I said to him. "Please! It's just—"

"What?"

"I can only stand – a little at a time. That's all."

He didn't answer me. He didn't take my hand again either. I felt a bit wild. I had a funny feeling, too. I couldn't walk properly. I wished he'd be nicer. More understanding. I did want him, I knew that now for sure. But what'd he be like, after? What'd I be like? I didn't want it to spoil everything. In a way I wished we could just have the trip without all these complications.

We got back to the camping site and wove through the other tents in the dark till we came to ours, four of them in a line. Then he turned round sharpish and faced me.

"I can't take much more of this," he said, very dramatic. "Boys can't, you know that."

Karen told me boys can't go without for more than a month or they go mad. She said that's why there's prostitutes. Of course I didn't exactly believe her. But he did look sort of crazy in the moonlight. I couldn't help being worried. What if me letting him touch me like that, and then making him stop, what if it really was bad for him? I didn't think it was very good for *me*, come to that.

"What do you want me to do?" I asked.

"Come into my tent with me. Now, quick, before the others come back."

"Oh no!" I said before I could think twice. Not that way. Not in a hurry, not with the rest of them tramping about and maybe peeping in.

And before he could say anything, I'd dived into my own tent, and tied the flap-tapes from the inside.

Forgot all about washing my gear.

11 · Old Erasmus

Couldn't go to sleep though. I kept thinking: *What am I getting in to? Should I or shouldn't I?* It was getting harder and harder not to. Saying no and keeping him off was upsetting me as well as him. Sometimes I wished we'd never started going together, necking and that. That we were just mates.

Once, when a bunch of us visited another school to play them at netball, they took us into their classroom and showed us this poster. I was fourteen then and it shocked me, to be honest – nothing like it in our school, you can bet. It would hardly go well with the crucifixes we had in every classroom.

It was headed CONTRACEPTION in big letters, and underneath, it had a bunch of boys drawn on one side and girls on the other. They all had think-balloons about what they thought of sex.

One of the boys was saying, "I wouldn't like to marry a girl who wasn't a virgin." He was Asian-looking and there was an Asian-looking girl saying, "I'm going to wait till I'm married." So *they* were all right, I mean provided they married each other.

But most of the other kids were thinking differently. One boy said, "If she loved me, she'd let me do it." But the girl we matched up with *him* was saying, "If he loved me, he wouldn't make me do it." And there was one girl saying, "I could never tell my parents." And another saying, "I'm afraid of getting pregnant." Well, we could see their point of view all right, at least I could.

I knew about the pill and that. And the other methods – well, sort of. Of course they taught us *nothing* about that in our school because the teachers were all Catholics, but you pick things up. I knew boys have this thing they can buy. What I didn't know was if Kev had any. No good getting myself into this hotel room and finding he hadn't. It might be too late then. I mean, when do they put them on? Soon enough so that if they don't, you can get out of doing it? I had an idea they put them on a bit late in the day, so to

88

speak. When copping out would be tricky.

I decided to ask Karen's advice. She's the expert, after all.

She came crawling in after a while. She whispered, "You awake?" I said yes. She said, "I'm not going to undress. I'm knackered." And crawled straight into her sleeping-bag.

After a bit I whispered, "Karen."

"What?"

"Did you really do it last night? With Cliff?"

"Mind your own business."

"I only wanted to know if he – I mean, if he'd brought – did he use those things?"

She rolled over in her bag to face me in the dark.

"Are *you* thinking of . . .?"

"Not with him!" I said before I thought.

"What's wrong with him?"

"You seemed to think there was something wrong, tonight."

"Oh, that. He turned me off, that's all. Wasn't his fault."

"Wasn't it?"

We stopped for a bit. I could hear the others laughing as they crawled into their tents. There was a shadow outside, and Michael's voice: "Early up, girls! We want to be in Rotterdam by lunchtime, or sooner." We called back, "Okay. 'Night."

Then I whispered to Karen, "Remember that chart thing? In that school, ages ago? About contraception?"

"Oh yeah – that. What about it?"

"Which of the girls was most like you?"

We'd all been playing which girls were us and which boys we'd like at the time. Not that we all told the truth. The one I thought was me then was saying, "I want to have a job first and enjoy myself." Now it was different.

"None of 'em was like me," Karen said. "I'd had a couple of boys by then. The schools wouldn't buy them charts if any of 'em had been saying what *I* think."

"What do you think?"

She was quiet a bit, making up her own think-balloon. Finally she said, "Sex is nicer than Yorkie bars."

I broke up. I had to half-smother myself in my sleeping-bag. At last I got hold of myself enough to say, "But you can't get in the family way from Yorkie bars."

"I'm on the pill," she said. She seemed proud of it.

"Does your mum know?"

"*My mum?* She'd kill me twice over if she did. I keep 'em in a tear in my mattress."

"Did you bring any?"

"Course I did."

After a long pause I said, "Karen."

"What?"

"Will you give me one?"

Now it was her started giggling. "You dumb-head," she said. "Do you think you just take one and go ahead and do it and you're safe? You got to take a whole course of 'em. It's got to change all your hormones before it can work."

"Oh," I said. Why couldn't they at least have told us *that* much at school? I felt a right goon, not knowing that. But now I did, I didn't much fancy having my hormones changed. Sounded much too drastic.

With her still sniggering away, I didn't feel like asking any more, for fear of making more of a twit of myself. Anyhow, how could she know if Kev had brought any of those things or not? And I certainly couldn't bring myself to ask, "Do they put them on at the beginning or the end?" So I just said, "'Night then."

But after a bit, she said, "Didn't your big sister tell you all about it?" And I said, "Mary's a virgin." And Karen said, "Must run in the family then. What about your mum?" And that set her off again.

Just before I dropped off to sleep, I remembered another couple on that poster, that we paired off. The boy was saying, "Why not? Everybody does." And the girl was saying, "I'm not going to do it just because the others do." I thought, *Well, that's sense anyway.* But when I went to sleep at last I didn't dream about Kev, or sex. I dreamt about eating Yorkie bars.

*

Michael got us on the road early next morning and even with a swim on the way we were in sight of Rotterdam by eleven o'clock.

I was glad we were going to sleep in a hostel that night. We hadn't overdone the washing bit in the camping sites, and I had a plastic bag full of undies that needed doing. My T-shirt was niffy. And my hair was a right mess, all full of dust and salt.

Kev cycled alongside me. He didn't say much and he didn't look at me much, but he did cycle with me. At our first sight of the tower blocks on the skyline he said, quietly, "That's our take-off point."

I didn't say a thing. Didn't commit myself.

We had to ride through a long tunnel to get into the city. Michael said it went under a huge river as wide as the Thames. I said I like water, but not on top of me. And I hate tunnels. I kept looking up to see if it was starting to drip through. If they ever build the Channel Tunnel you won't catch me going in it – all those tons and tons of water overhead, it just doesn't make sense. We rode through single file with the traffic roaring past. Thank heaven for the cycle-track! I swerved so often looking up at the roof, I'd have been killed for sure if we'd been on the roadway.

When we were safely through, Michael led us off the main road and into a bunch of side streets and then pulled up at a little shop where you could get postcards. We all bought some. I got five, mostly country views of dykes and windmills and that, but one of this Euromast tower we were meant to be going up. I was looking forward to that.

One of the postcards on sale caught my eye and I picked it up. It was some kind of statue. I kept staring at it. I didn't want to buy it – I mean not to send; I could just imagine how Sean or Lily would send me up – but I kept staring at it just the same. Finally I took it to Michael, who was buying us each a map of the city.

"What's this thing?"

"Why don't you look at the back?"

I did, and it said something in Dutch of course. "Can't read it."

A Dutch lady was standing near us. "It is called *Destroyed City*. It was put up to remind us of the bombing."

"When was that then?" Kev asked her. He loves anything about the war, especially planes and bombs and air-raids and that.

"In May 1940," she said, "the Germans completely destroyed our city, isn't it?" Karen giggled at her funny English. "There was nothing left. Just ashes, and—" She stopped and looked at Michael.

"Ruins," he said.

"Ah, yes. But one thing still stood after all the bombs. It was another statue, the statue of Erasmus." She showed us another postcard. This had an ordinary statue on it of a man in a priest's robe holding a book.

"Like St Paul's in London," said Michael. "Just stood there all by itself in the rubble."

"Something always survives, isn't it?" said the lady. She smiled at us and left the shop.

Kev was buying something at the counter, and now he put it in his pocket and turned round. "Come on, let's go. I want my lunch," he said.

We paid for our postcards. I bought the extra one, the *Destroyed City* one. I just wanted it. I couldn't decide whether I liked it or hated it. It was a figure of a man with his arms reaching up and a great hole through his middle. All his arms and legs were very thick and clumsy – he didn't look like a real man. But he looked as if he was putting up his arms to catch the bombs or stop them dropping on him. Only why the hole? I hate these modern statues really; I liked the other one she showed us – the man with the book – much better. So why didn't I buy that one then, if I was so keen on statues all of a sudden?

We got back on our bikes and rode through into the main part of the town. After what that lady said I'd half expected to find a lot of empty spaces, but of course it had all been built up again. Lots of it was just about like London. There were parks and that, and wide clean streets. We went in to a little snack-bar for lunch, and this time I did have some of the apple sauce with my pork chop (I felt like lashing out a bit) and it wasn't bad. The boys all had some Dutch lager. Con had special onion soup with cheese on top. She fairly lapped it up and then had an open sandwich with heaven knows what on it, and loads of mayonnaise. She wouldn't give me even a nibble, she said it was too good to spare.

While we were eating, some of us were writing our postcards, but Kev wasn't. He'd borrowed Darryl's guide-book and was bent over a map it had.

"What you looking for?" I asked him.

"The railway station."

I got all goosebumps. "Oh go on! Let's look at this town first."

He looked up at me. His blue eyes had gone all sort of burning.

"If you don't want to come with me, just say. I can go on my own, you know, easy."

"But what d'you want to leave the rest of us for, I mean if—" I could feel myself getting red— "if I don't go?"

"I told you. I heard Amsterdam's great, the clubs and that."

"If you mean strip-tease clubs, I'm not going to them even if I do come."

He looked at me a bit longer and then slammed the book shut and gave it back to Darryl. "Please yourself," he said. "But we could have a good time, you and me, Trace, without doing nothing you don't want to do." And he squeezed my knee under the table.

Well. What was I to make of that? *If he loved me, he wouldn't make me do it.* Did he mean it, or was it just a come-on? I wished I knew.

Michael had been looking at his map, too. He had a lot of things he wanted to see, and that meant us seeing them as well, unless we wanted to lose him. He did get a bit bossyguts then, I must say, with his "We've got to see this" and "We mustn't miss that". We all wanted to see the docks with the big ships and the cranes and all that, and the tower, but when it came to museums we weren't so keen.

In the end we compromised. He suggested a boat tour, which would take us all round the city on the rivers and canals, and we jumped at that of course – even Con, who I thought had been looking a bit restless. Funny, I didn't want Con to take off and leave us. When she got restless, I did.

When we were going down to the harbour to find the tourist boats, we suddenly saw this huge *thing*. Big and black against the sky. Gave us all a turn. It was the *Destroyed City* man. He was much bigger than I'd thought from looking at the picture. You could see the sky through the big hole in his body. He gave me the shivers, honest. He was all black and twisted as if he'd been burned, and his arms were much too long.

"Look!" shouted Cliff. "If it ain't the Incredible Hulk!"

I hoped Kev wouldn't laugh, but he did. "Poor old Hulk," he said. "He must be done for this time. Somebody shot a cannonball through him."

"That's where his heart's been torn out," said Michael.

He said it so quiet I think only Con and me heard. We both looked at him, then back at the statue. Of course I saw straight away now why the hole was there. I still thought it was a horrible-looking thing, but at least it made sense, not like some of that rubbish that's just lumps and they call it *Concept* or *Infinity* or some other mad name. Still, I couldn't wait to get away and I was glad Michael seemed in a hurry too.

"Come on, we'll just catch the next boat."

The boat tour was great. We saw the port properly, from the water. The boys loved it, specially the big radar thing that helps the ships come in in a fog. But it didn't take long, and the minute we stepped ashore Michael was off again about his museums and something called "Bow Centrum". When we asked him what it was, he said it was all about town planning and architecture and that. We all let out a groan that was more like a howl.

"Nobody's getting me to no town planning exhibition," Cliff said.

"Nor to a museum," said Kev. "Blimey. Only poufs go to museums."

"I go to 'em," said Michael. "You calling me a pouf?"

Kev grunted something. Con said, "What kind of museum is it? I'm not going if it's paintings and that, but I don't mind if it's science." (She's brilliant at science subjects.)

"There's all kinds," said Michael. "Look, why don't we split up for a bit? You all go and do whatever you want, and we'll meet at the youth hostel." He made us open up the maps he'd bought us and he drew a circle round the youth hostel where we were supposed to sleep. He pointed out some of the main places, and made a few helpful suggestions. Then he said, "No one coming with me then?" And he was on his way.

Suddenly Kev, who'd been looking at his map, said, "Yeah, I'll come. And Tracy. Come on, Trace, let's have a butcher's at this Bow whatchamacallit." I nearly fainted. Kev had howled louder than any of us when Michael first mentioned the place. What was he up to? Anyway I decided to go, and we set off on our bikes, leaving the other four looking a bit lost.

It was a fair way to where we were going, and, when I checked my map later, I found Michael had cheated a bit. He didn't go straight to the Bow whatsit. He took us all round the mulberry bush, looking at this and that. None of it grabbed me (and Kev was getting really narked) until we came into a square and I suddenly saw this statue – not the *Destroyed City* one, the other, the one of the man in the robe.

We stopped beside it, or rather under it. Kev was grunting and groaning as if he had a bad belly-ache by then.

"What we stopping for? Why the hell don't we get on with it?"

"Let's just see this," I said. "He was on that postcard."

Kev muttered something that sounded like "sod the bleeding postcard" and just leaned on his bike looking the other way and heaving great sighs every two minutes. But Michael had his guide-book out.

"It's Erasmus," he said.

"Oh yeah," I said, not to show my ignorance. I stood off a bit. What I liked best was the way the statue looked as if he was just turning a page of his book. If you stood there long enough, you felt as if you'd see him do it.

Michael was reading. *"Call a spade a spade!"* he said suddenly.

"Eh?"

"He was the first person who said that."

"I call a spade a black bastard," said Kev. We both looked at him. He turned round, saw us looking, and went red. "Just a joke," he shouted.

Michael went back to his book. "Listen to this," he said slowly, and read it out: *"Since the human race insists upon being completely crazy; since everybody from the pope down to the humblest of village priests, from the richest of men to the most miserable paupers, from the fine lady in her silks and satins down to the slut in her calico dressing-gown—"*

"Oh, I like her! Specially the dressing-gown," said Kev, sarcastic. "Are we going to stop here all day listening to this load of rubbish?"

Michael read right on, taking no notice.

"Since the whole world has set its heart against using its God-given brain but insists upon letting itself be entirely guided by its greed, its vanity and its ignorance—"

"Speak for your bleeding self, you silly old twot!" muttered Kev.

"—why in the name of a reasonable Deity should the few truly intelligent people waste so much of their time and effort in trying to change the human race into something it never wanted to be? Let them be happy in their follies. Do not deprive them of that which gives them more satisfaction than anything else, their sovereign power to make fools of themselves."

By this time Kev was pretty near dancing with rage. In spite of himself he'd been listening, and he chose to take what old Erasmus had said as a personal insult.

"And I suppose you agree with all that!" he yelled at Michael. "You know what that is, don't you? That's bloody Fascism, that's what that is. He means us when he says ignorant and greedy and that – us Catholics—"

"Oh, come on!" said Michael. "He doesn't only mean—"

"Pope and priests! That's what it said. Or, okay, not only Catholics, but ordinary people, working classes and that – us! Setting himself up above us, saying we're not worth bothering about! Silly old shithouse! I'd like to kick his head in—"

"You're a bit late, he's been dead getting on for five hundred years."

That brought Kev up short. He stopped jumping about and yelling and just stood there looking up at this statue of Erasmus, standing there so calm, the way he'd been all through the bombing, reading his book and paying no attention to anybody.

I couldn't help agreeing with Kev in a way. Old Erasmus was like some of the teachers we had. They taught us because it was their job, but you could tell they didn't reckon us. There was one, old Sullivan, he'd been teaching for forty years he told us once, and he reckoned he'd got something into the heads of maybe a dozen kids. For the rest he just stuck the stuff in front of us day after day and if we wanted it we could take it and if we didn't, well, it was no skin off of his nose, he'd done his best.

And the truth was, now I thought about it, none of us did take it, not more than a quarter of what he offered us. But whose fault was it? Dad would say it was ours for not trying harder. Mum always blames something called "society" for everything. Sean agrees with her, but then he's a born moaner. Vlady never blames anybody. He just gets on with it.

Me? Well, I don't know, do I? But one thing I did think of, all by myself, standing there waiting for the old fellow to turn his next page. I thought, *He's got stuck. He'll never turn it. They're all stuck, all them cleverdicks, they don't know what to do about us*. Erasmus said, "Turn your backs on them, they're no good, you're wasting your time." Some of them go on trying, like Barry, our form teacher, he kept on at us trying to shove in a bit of culture, but we just sent him up. We didn't want to know.

Michael did, though. He wanted to know. He even wanted to give us some of what he was finding out. It was that that made Kev mad, Michael spouting at him. It was Michael Kev wanted to bash in, not old Erasmus at all – I saw that suddenly from the way he'd stopped looking up at the statue and started glaring at Michael.

"Here. I've had enough of this!" he said. "Are we going or aren't we? Come on, Trace."

Michael didn't say a thing. He put his guide-book away and got astride his bike without looking at either of us. I got ready to move on too. Then all of a sudden, just as we were off, it happened.

Kev dropped his bike on its side, pack and all, reached into his pocket and then made a run at the statue. It was standing on a big square lump of stone with lots of writing printed on it. Kev stood there for a minute, doing something. He was blocking our view. Michael just had time to say, "What you doing?" when Kev stepped aside and we could see.

What he must've bought in that shop was one of those thick-nib felt pens – a black one, the kind they use for notices. In big letters, just under Erasmus's feet, he'd scrawled the word:

CRAP

Michael's not a fast mover, only sometimes. Like now. Now he moved so fast I hardly saw him. His bike crashed over as he jumped. He grabbed Kev by the front of his T-shirt and gave him two smacks round the head.

"Rub it off! Rub it off!" he kind of ground out between his teeth. He was shaking Kev back and forth so I thought his neck'd snap. Actually it was the worst thing he could have done.

Because we weren't the only people in the square of course,

there were hundreds of them coming and going. Maybe nobody would have noticed what Kev had done, but they couldn't help noticing Michael having a go at him. Straight away they stopped, half a dozen of them, and stared, and I knew in another second some of them would try to interfere, and the next thing, they'd see that word written on their statue. In Holland that's probably enough to get you put away for life.

I grabbed Michael's shirt from behind and pulled it practically off him.

"Michael! Come on! Come away!"

He dropped Kev and turned to me. His face was all funny, screwed up like a kid's and bright red under his red hair.

"We got to get it off!"

"You start scrubbing at it, they'll know we done it!"

"I don't care—" And he made a move towards the statue.

I stepped in front of him. Like that I covered the word with my body. Nobody'd seen it yet. There was getting to be a crowd round us now so I kept my voice very quiet.

"You come near this statue and I'm going to scream my head off. I mean it."

That stopped him. Quick as I could I went on, "Tonight when it's dark we'll come back and get it off somehow. *Please* Michael! It won't do any good if you get in trouble. We need you!"

He looked at me for half a minute. I'd got the statue and the word behind me and all kinds of bother in front. But for those few seconds it was just Michael's eyes looking into mine. Then he grabbed my wrist and pulled.

"Get on your bike."

Funny thing was, I didn't want to move. I didn't want the word to show. It was like not wanting to undress in public. Kev wasn't just someone that I could pretend I didn't know. He was my boyfriend. I felt ashamed of what he'd done. I didn't want anyone to see it, and that wasn't just being scared of bother.

Michael and me just stood like that, looking at each other. When a red-haired person goes "hot and cold" you can see it in their skin. Michael saw why I wouldn't move and he saw it made sense. He stood there till people got bored and moved away. But he was going hot and cold the whole time and so was I.

At last things looked clear and he said, "Come on."

We grabbed up our bikes and shot off across the square.

Kev had a head start. I'd never seen him ride so fast. But with Michael and me on racers, we soon caught him up.

Michael zoomed past him like a police-car in a film, and forced him to pull up.

"I got a word to say to you, Kevin."

Kev stood astride his bike and looked this way and that. There'd been a bit of larking since we started the trip, one sort or another, but Michael had never sounded like that before, even when Kev went into the water that time.

"You're a vandal," Michael said. "There's nothing I can do about that. So be a vandal in Acton, it won't notice there – half the population under twenty's at it with their felt pens and their spray-cans, mucking up every decent bit of clean paint and brick-work in the area. What they do it for I'll never know – unless it's the only way they got of making their mark in this world. But I hate it. I hate litter and I hate graffiti and I hate vandalism. Most of all I hate idiots like you."

Kev's face swung back to him. He's thin, Kev, and now all the bones stuck out on his cheeks and round his jaw, white. I could see him gripping the handlebars of his bike. I knew he wanted to bash Michael but he didn't dare and it was killing him. It was killing me too. Michael was asking for it, going on like that. I moved my bike closer to Kev's without thinking.

"You want to bring your lousy habits to someone else's country," Michael went on, "go ahead! I hope you wind up in porridge. You can rot there for all I care! Just try not to take Tracy with you."

He gave me a look then, a different look. Angry, but not at me – more sort of *for* me.

"She's worth ten of you," he said to Kev.

I thought of something then, all right. A brick bridge over a railway, with some words sprayed on it in white paint.

"No, I ain't!" I shouted. "You let him alone! Who d'you think you are, anyway? Michael the bloody archangel?"

There was a silence. Then, all of a sudden, Michael seemed to calm down. He looked at the ground, so we only saw the top of his carrot head. He'd been shaking, but now he seemed to stop himself, forced himself to relax. When he looked at us again, his face wasn't red any more.

"All right," he said. "Let's go to the Bouwcentrum."

"I ain't going nowhere with you," said Kev.

His voice was different – low and dangerous. A hard man's voice.

"I only come with you 'cause I saw on the map that that place is near the railway station. Trace and me's going to Amsterdam. We'll see you Tuesday on the boat. Come on, Trace." And he started wheeling his bike past Michael.

Michael let him go, but when I followed he put his hand on my arm.

"Don't go with him, Tracy. Please. Stop with the rest of us."

But I was feeling what Kev was feeling. Hurt, ashamed. Put down. I hated Michael for that.

"Him and me's together," I said. "Maybe you're better than us. But we're as good as each other, anyway."

And I got on my bike and rode off after Kev without looking back once.

12 · Blue Room

The Dutch train ran across the flat Dutch country. I sat holding
Kev's hand too tight and thinking to myself in time to the wheels,
I must, I must, like Amsterdam. I must, I must, like Amsterdam.
I was facing the engine-end of the train and I kept looking ahead
all the time. I didn't want to look back. Or think back. It was
hard not to – hard to help wondering what Con'd think when she
heard we'd gone, and of the fun the others'd have in the youth
hostel that night. Where would *I* be that night? I didn't want to
think of that either. So I just tried to think of Amsterdam, and
discos, and nice food. And being alone with Kev, and him being
nice to me because I'd stuck to him and stood up for him to
Michael.

Pity, though, never going up that Euromast tower. . . .

It was about four o'clock when we got there. We got our bikes
and gear off and lugged them into the main hall of the station.
Looking out the windows I could see water, lots of it, and it
made me feel better somehow. Kev was dead quiet. He'd hardly
opened his mouth the whole way. Now I took a look at him,
wheeling our bikes across the first of about a thousand bridges.
He didn't look good. It was an hour and a half, about, since his
row with Michael but he was still white and screwed-up looking.

"Kev?"

"Yeah?"

"D'you feel bad or something? What's wrong?"

"Nothing! Lemme alone."

We walked a bit further. The big canal had loads of boats and
barges on it. Along its edges were big brick houses with all
different fronts. Some of the high roofs kind of went up in steps
at the edges and others had curvy bits, or like scrolls. They
looked ever so old. There was a big old tower, too, on the edge of
the water. I wondered what that was . . . Michael would know,
with his guide-book at the ready . . .

We rode about the streets for about an hour without really

101

knowing where we were heading. If I hadn't been sort of upset and uncomfortable about us being here and about Kev acting so quiet and strange, I think I'd have liked Amsterdam better than Rotterdam. I like old places best. Not grotty old places like Horn Lane with its horrible dirty old houses with the windows broken and the gardens all gone wild and full of rubbish, but old buildings and that, that've been kept up. There were whole squares of them here. One or two looked like palaces. There were loads of statues. We even saw a nice one of Jesus. They'd done his halo like a plate on the back of his head. I thought that was a bit silly, but then how *do* you do a halo out of stone? Anyway Kev wouldn't let me stop to look at things much. I had to pretend to be checking my tyres or doing something to my rucksack if I wanted to have a look at a view down a canal from a bridge or a nice building or something. He just shot on without looking back.

Finally I caught him up by the side of one of the smaller canals. It had trees leaning over it, and there were little cafés where you could sit outside. I was nearly fainting from hunger by then, so I said: "Let's stop and eat, eh?"

He grunted, but he got off and propped his bike against a wall with about a dozen others. I looked at the cafés. One of them had a little sign on it which said *Tourist Menu*. Michael had told us you could get cheaper grub at them.

"Aren't you hungry?"

"I dunno."

He still hadn't looked at me.

We sat at one of the outdoor tables. The sun was still quite high and the water of the canal was gold. The street between us and it was narrow and cobbled. There wasn't much traffic, just the odd van and bike. It was ever so nice, especially when the waiter brought us fried eggs on a big slice of bread and butter with some ham in between. Mine was gone in two minutes. I drank my soup next – tomato – and then there was pears and ice-cream. Food's great for making you forget your troubles. Till I got through that lot, I half forgot Kev.

But when I did look to see how he was getting on, he'd only picked. I was still hungry, but it seemed heartless to ask if I could have his bread and ham, and his pears (he'd eaten the ice-cream and the egg). Still, it seemed a shame to waste them.

"You got a pain, Kev, or what? Why don't you finish?"

"I don't feel like it."

"Can I have it?"

"What you got in there, a bottomless pit?"

That sounded more like him, so I grinned at him and he grinned back, a bit anyway.

"What's wrong?" I asked him. "Cheer up."

"Yeah," he said. "We're here, after all. We got here, like I planned."

He seemed to perk up then, and ate his ham with his fingers.

"What we going to do?" I asked, though in a way I didn't want to know. The sun was just creeping down now, behind the houses with their funny Dutch fronts, and I couldn't help starting to think about that hotel room.

He was thinking about it too. "We'll find a hotel first," he said, "then we'll go out somewhere."

"Kev."

"What?"

"Are you sure you can afford a hotel?"

Now he looked straight at me and put his hand on my knee.

"You want to see something?"

"What?"

He unzipped his jacket and reached into his inside pocket. He took out his wallet. Then he looked all round, cautious. There were people at other tables, mostly young students and that, but nobody was noticing us, so he opened the wallet like a book and showed me what was stuck behind the top flap.

I nearly fell over. He had about sixty, maybe seventy pound in there, in tenners. He flipped through them slowly, just the edges, to show me. He was watching my face. Then he put the wallet away. He looked ever so much better now.

"Your dad never give you all that!" I found I was whispering, I don't know why.

"I told you. I worked."

"You was only off school a few odd days," I said. "How could you earn so much?"

"Never you mind!" he said. He snapped his fingers for the waiter, like you see them do in films, and ordered beers. I felt dead worried all of a sudden.

"Kev! You never nicked it!"

"Naaa! Course not."

"Then how?"

"I did a little job for some blokes. Don't fret about it. You and me's going to have a good time."

My mouth was all dry. I didn't like it. All that money! Like I said in the beginning, I'm not all that fussy. I mean everybody breaks the law now and again. But that's not to say I agree with being *dishonest*.

"Kev, I want to know how you got it."

He gave one of his sighs.

"Look. There's these blokes, see, friends of my uncle's. They deal in bikes mainly, second-hand bikes, and other things sometimes, electrical. Cassettes and that, and the odd telly. I got my bike from them. What I do, I spend the odd day going round the second-hand shops and markets, flogging these things for 'em. They drive me in their van and then I go in with whatever they give me, and I bring 'em the money, and they give me a commission. They got a pitch at Southall Market and one in Portobello and other ones here and there, and I help 'em sell and they pay me."

"*All that?* For just a few days?"

"Well, I been doing it a few months now. I been saving," he said. Ever so virtuous.

Did I believe it was all on the up and up? Did I? I don't know. I wanted to. He was looking me in the eye. I thought; *If I had a Bible now, I could make him swear, like Mum used to*. Yes. I remember thinking that. So I must have had my doubts. And now I think about it, I distinctly remember he said, "I did a little job". *A* job, one. Sixty pound for one "little" job? Who did he think he was kidding?

Me. And he did, too. If I hadn't fancied him, and run away with him, and said what I had to Michael, I wouldn't have let myself believe. But I had. So I did.

And once I'd let myself believe that that money was okay, I had to believe Kev was straight too. All ways straight. That's why, when we finished our grub and he said, "Let's go," I got up quiet and got on my bike and followed him like a good little

104

puppy-dog till he stopped at a small yellow building with a sticking-out sign saying *HOTEL*.

He hesitated a bit on the step. Then he turned to me.

"Just remember, we're married," he said.

That gave me a start all right. I hadn't thought I'd have to tell lies. I didn't think they bothered with all that nowadays, but we did look a bit young to be shacking up together. Come to that, if I'd been running a hotel I wouldn't have let us across the doorstep, the way we looked. Kev was all over wavy white salt-marks from where the sea-water had dried on his jeans; his hair stuck up in spikes and he had this bit of a stubble four days old. As for me, I was a mess as well, and I think one reason I went in with him was the idea of finding a nice bathroom to wash my hair and gear and get cleaned up. I didn't look much beyond that.

Anyway, nobody stopped us, though the fat woman behind the reception desk gave us a funny look. I'd thought you'd have to sign a book (they always do in films), but she just gave us a key with a tag on it. Our number was 8. I'll always remember that number.

We were told we could leave our bikes in a garage place at the back. We took them round there and unloaded them and went in the hotel again through the back door. We looked at the room numbers on the doors and found ours on the first floor. Kev unlocked the door. I couldn't hardly breathe as we went in.

It was just as I'd pictured – a nice clean little room with twin beds with bright blue covers (I can never see that blue without thinking of Holland) and a long window with a little balcony outside. I went straight to that. The sun was going down behind the old buildings. You could see the canals, sometimes a whole curve of one, sometimes just a glint between two walls. There were trees in the streets and lots of plants everywhere – window boxes and that, and "curtain-plants" in every window. Even our hotel room had a little plant-basket in it. It hung from a hook in the ceiling, and the leaves spilled down. I touched them as I turned back into the room. They were heart-shaped. Seemed like a good omen.

Kev said, "Well girl, we're here. Like it?"

His bad mood had gone. He was full of beans. Suddenly (well, you can't help what comes into your head) I remembered a seaside postcard that one of Sean's mates sent him once from Margate. It was of a bridegroom and a best man coming out of church and the best man says, "Are you nervous?" and the bridegroom says, "I never felt more *cocksure* in my life." It sat on our breakfast-room mantelpiece two months, till someone went and told Dad what it meant and he ripped it up. . . . What'd I have to think of that now for? I wanted to feel romantic and that, I mean if we were really going to do it. . . . But looking at Kev, grinning away – well, cocksure was the word for him, take it how you like.

I said, "Yeah, it's really nice."

"Bet you weren't expecting nothing like this," he said, strutting round the room, picking up ashtrays and stuff, like he'd just bought the place. Suddenly he looked closer at something in his hand.

"Here, look at this!" he said, laughing, and gave it to me.

It was a little po-shaped thing, blue again. Painted round the edge, in English, in tiny curly writing, it had:

Honourably pinched from the Parkstaat Hotel, Amsterdam.

Somehow that gave me a lift. Kev liked it too. While we were laughing together he put his arms round me.

Okay, we started necking. It was nice, but the beds sort of got in the way. I kept thinking; *It's not just a matter of necking this time.* When he tried to make me sit down on the edge, I wouldn't.

"Listen. I'm going to have a bath and wash my hair. Then I'm going to put some clean gear on. Then we're going out."

"Out? Who says?"

"You wanted to go to some of the clubs. So let's go!"

He brightened up. "Okay!"

I lay in the bath a long time. I was thinking. If only it could all seem like *fun,* sex and that. Why should it all be so serious, so kind of heavy? It's our religion that makes it seem like that. Getting it all mixed up with sin. Deep down I knew that was what was holding me back – the idea of being a sinner. Apart from maybe Kev making a mess of it somehow, giving me a baby or even just not being nice to me, after.

I lay there in the lovely warm water and I felt all the biking aches floating away, *and* the aches from the row with Michael and the Erasmus business. I closed my eyes and thought of the little dark heart-shaped leaves and the blue bed-covers and the po with the funny message, which really said, "You can nick me and take me home and not feel guilty." Could I do it with Kev and not feel guilty? How can you know how you'll feel after?

I thought of K ren. Once, before she started saying "Mind your own business" to everything, she told me *her* first time was in a garden shed. Now that's what I call sordid. Only, what? Now she can think of sex as being like something sweet to eat, lovely while you're having it but not important. "Naughty but nice" like the ad for the cream cakes says. I *wished* I felt like that. I thought, *Maybe the way to get to feel like it is, to do it so often you have to stop worrying.*

I didn't want to move from that bath, ever. As long as I stayed there, locked in and floating in the warm water, I was safe. I washed my hair. Every time I did, some more of that dye came out. All the water was pale brown by the time I finished. I lay there a few minutes more, but I was getting cold. I got out and straight away I started shivering. I just didn't want to go back into that bedroom, somehow.

There was one more thing I had to do, and that was wash out my pants and socks and that. I wondered if I should ask Kev if I could wash anything for him. I decided not to. After all, we *weren't* married.

I looked at myself in the mirror. When you stop being a virgin, it's one of the biggest changes in your life. Would I look different to myself, by tomorrow? My hair was growing out a bit, and getting fairer. I thought of how Dad had looked at me when I'd gone punk, and he saw how I'd changed. Even a little change like that had frightened me. . . .

I got dressed quickly and carried all my stuff into the bedroom.

Kev was lying on one of the beds with his shoes on. He hadn't turned back the cover, even off the pillow.

"You shouldn't lie on the bed in your mucky gear," I said before I could stop myself.

"What's it matter? They got to wash it after every customer

anyhow."

"How long we going to be here?"

"Till the cash runs out. . . . Unless I can find a way to make some more," he added.

"Go and have a bath," I said.

"What do I want a bath for?"

But I wasn't having that. "Go on, I'm not going out with you like that!" *Nor stopping in neither,* I said to myself.

He groaned, but he took himself off. I hung my wet things over the balcony rail. Hoped none of them would blow off, but there was no wind. Then I just stood there again, fluffing my hair with my fingers to dry it.

The lights were coming on now. I felt better. *Why not,* I thought, *why not? It's got to happen sometime. What if I just took all my clothes off and lay down in the bed and waited till he came back, all clean from his bath, and just – got it over with?* But I couldn't.

I couldn't.

It's got to overtake me, I thought. *He's got to make it happen, he's got to make me want it so I can't help myself. Tonight. It'll happen tonight.*

13 · Nightlife

When it came to where we were to go, of course neither of us had a clue. So we thought we'd ask. But who? The only one we could think of was that fat lady at reception. Only she didn't look the sort who went to night clubs much.

But anyway we went down to the desk. From the top of the stairs we could see it wasn't her. It was a dark young bloke. Looked like a Paki.

Kev doesn't like Pakis.

"I see they come choco and coffee flavoured here too," he said, quite loud.

Of course he didn't think this man would understand English. He didn't say it to hurt him. He just says things like that. Still, I gave him a nudge. Always reminds me how I feel about the Irish and Polish jokes, cracks like that about blacks.

The Paki (or whatever he was) didn't look up from his book. Kev went up to him.

"Night club?" he said, rather loud.

Now he looked up, all smiles.

"A night club? Certainly, sir. What kind do you prefer?"

Perfect English. God! Still . . . probably didn't hear. I hoped not.

Kev said, "Something special, but not too dear."

"Of course, I know the very place. It is called *Achteras*. That means in English, 'Back Axle'. As on a car. A witty name, isn't it?"

I thought it was a dead silly name for a nightclub, but of course I didn't say so. It turned out not to be very far away – we needn't take our bikes. We could just stroll along the canal, across some bridges, and there we were.

It was down in a cellar which I thought made it more exciting. You went down a passage all painted green with gold stars to a table where a blond man was taking money. I thought he was a bit old still to have such lovely golden hair, but he smiled at us in

109

a very friendly way and said, "Good evening, dears." I suppose he knew from our T-shirts we were English. We could hear the music booming away very near us. Kev paid. It was about £5 each just to get in.

We opened the double doors. The music bashed out at us.

It was nearly pitch black at first; every few seconds lights flashed on and off again in patterns. One spotlight kept sweeping the room. Every sweep it was a new colour, mostly pinks and violets.

It was a big place. There wasn't a proper stage, just an open space in the middle of the tables, with a group playing straight rock. The singer was a woman. She looked rather old for a pop singer, and she hadn't much of a figure. She wore an old-fashioned long fitted dress in a spangly material, and she was crooning out a song in a low, rather hard voice. All round her were couples dancing.

We groped our way to a free table. My eyes took about five minutes to get used to the dark. There was something funny about those people. Kev caught on before I did.

"Bloody hell!" he muttered suddenly. "They're all men!"

"Who are?"

"All of 'em. The lot. The women too. They're *men*."

I looked round again, in a sort of panic. I couldn't be the only girl in the place! There was the singer for a start. . . . But one really good look at her hefty shoulders and hard, jutting jaw showed me my mistake.

I looked round at the tables near us. There were couples sitting with their heads together over their drinks, whispering and laughing . . . some of them weren't even dressed as women, they were sitting there necking or holding hands with men and *they* were men. Kev was right. I could see that now – even the ones with blond wigs and high heels and split skirts.

I felt as if I'd wandered into the gents by mistake – no, worse than that. As if I'd got into a world where there were no women except me. Why had they let me in? Why wasn't I stopped at the door?

"They're all bloody poufs," muttered Kev. He started to get up to go. Suddenly a big fellow in leather trousers and a plaid shirt open to the waist, with very short hair and a black moustache, came up to our table. He had leather wristlets studded with brass nails, and he looked harder than Kojak without his lollypop.

"Commie dancin'," he said (or that's what it sounded like). And he wasn't talking to me, either.

Kev stared at him with his mouth open. Then he sat down again, quick. "Er – no thanks," he said, and shook his head till I thought he'd shake it off.

The man held his great meaty arms out. Kev seemed to shrink till he was nearly under the table.

"Vy not?" he asked. "Pretty little Englishman. Kom."

"Bloody hell," muttered Kev. He'd gone sort of putty coloured. Then he had an inspiration. He turned to me. "I'm with her."

The big butch fellow looked at me.

"Ah yes," he said. "Very nice boy. Excuse." And he waved to me and pushed his great hairy chest through the crowd.

Then I knew why old golden boy had let me in. He thought I was a fella.

"I want to go," I whispered.

"Good thinking," said Kev.

We pushed our way out. The old poufter gave us a look. "Something not nice?"

"No, no! It's all very nice," said Kev, with a sickly smile. "Just not our scene, that's all." And we ran for it along the green corridor and up the steps into the street.

"Of course the little black bastard heard me," said Kev after a bit.

"Who?"

"The one at the hotel. He heard what I said. That's why he sent us to that queer club. Ten quid down the drain! I'd like to kick his teeth in."

I don't know what got into me then, but I stopped feeling faintly sick and started wanting to laugh. Kev's face when that macho type came up to him for a dance! I just started to giggle and I couldn't stop.

"What's the flaming joke?" Kev nearly shouted. "I don't think it's funny! I don't think it should be allowed!"

"Go on, it's their club. They can do what they like, they weren't hurting nobody."

"I thought that Hell's Angel was going to do me an injury. And what about that singer? Poor man's Danny La Rue."

"Get away, there's no law against a bit of dressing up. It was a good laugh if you ask me."

We were walking back beside the canal. Kev was striding along. I didn't like the look in his eye. He can turn nasty when he wants. I once saw him pull a pen-knife on a black boy at school who threw a punch at him.

"You know what it says in the Bible about that sort of 'dressing up' as you call it," he said.

"No, what?"

"Stoning to death. That's what."

I stopped walking.

"Get away!" I said.

"Straight up."

"Jesus never said that!"

"Jesus! Who's talking about Jesus? It's in the Old Testament, isn't it!"

Is it? I never read much of the Old Testament. Only Adam and Eve and that. And Noah.

I came up again level with him.

"Listen, Kev, let's try somewhere else."

"I'm going to settle that Paki first."

My heart nearly stopped. Not a fight! I grabbed his arm.

"Kev, don't start anything in there – *please*! I'm sure he didn't mean any harm—"

"He meant it all right. But he'll be sorry when I've done with him."

"Kev—"

No use. He'd got himself worked into such a state he started to run. I ran after him, but he got ahead of me, and by the time I got to our little hotel he'd gone in the door.

I rushed in, my heart in my mouth. There was Kev, leaning over the counter. He'd got hold of this little dark man, and was shouting at him.

"What you think I am, Cocoa? Think I'm a pouf, do you? Well, I'll tell you what you are, you're a little black turd, that's what! I'm going to bash your face in for you—"

He'd've done it too, if I hadn't jumped on him and dragged

him off. I had to give his arm a good knock to make him let go, but I'm quite strong when I need to be and he wasn't going to hit me. And of course there was the counter in between too, and the other man was struggling to get away. Anyway I got Kev off and stood in front of him and said, "That's enough!" Then I said to the Paki, "I'm sorry, but you shouldn't have sent us to that place. Now please tell us a good place to go, and we'll go to it."

The poor man was rubbing his neck and straightening his shirt. He looked really shaken. He said, "You can try the Greenhouse. It is cheap with a good floorshow. If you don't like it, don't blame me. You English have strange tastes. And strange behaviours." And he rubbed his neck again and glared at Kev.

Well, you couldn't help seeing his point. I almost heaved Kev out the door before anything else could happen.

We went to this Greenhouse place. It turned out to be miles off. We had to get a bus in the end. I was half starved by now, and I'd have settled for a good meal, but Kev had the bit between his teeth. He was going to see a rude floorshow if it killed both of us. And it nearly did.

Again he shelled out. This time at least we stopped long enough to get a drink and a bite to eat. It was only a bite, and all – scraps of something wrapped up in bacon, and some nuts, I ask you! I could have put away four Tourist Menus and had room left over for a couple of quarterpounders.

It wasn't as if I had much company in my misery, either. Kev just sat there drumming the little table with his fingers, staring at the band with his jaw-muscles working, just daring them not to bring on something worth writing home about. Me, I was dreading it, to say the true. I'd seen the pictures in Soho, and a time or two on late-night telly when Mum wasn't around to switch off, and I thought I'd just as soon give it a miss. Tonight of all nights, when I was trying to get into a romantic mood, sex in the raw wasn't really what I was after.

It was what I got though. Blimey O'Reilly! Near the knuckle wasn't in it, it was right through to the elbow. The poufs were a convent tea-party by comparison, in fact before long I was wishing I was back at the old Back Axle watching them all having a dance and a bit of a cuddle, while that dear old poufter in his cover-up dress and fur stole squawked away into the mike. . . . Well, to be honest, after a bit I just shut my eyes and spared my blushes. I swear if I hadn't, it might have screwed up my sex-life for life.

"Here," Kev said suddenly. "We might as well go. It's no fun with you sitting there with your face in the ashtray."

So that was another tenner up the spout *and* we had to get a taxi back to the hotel, which put Kev into a bad temper again. It was ever so late. I had an awful feeling the hotel would be shut. That was all we needed.

But it wasn't. The light was still on in the sign. I remember the relief. Little did I know!

As we went into the hall, we saw her straight away. The fat lady. She was standing behind the reception counter with her arms folded. She had her hair done in a roll, like a yellow balloon tyre round her head and down over her forehead. Her eyebrows went straight across. Frightening. *And* her jaw stuck out.

We started for the stairs, but she spoke to us. What a voice! Like every hard teacher we ever had rolled up in one.

"*Yust* one minute please!"

We stopped dead.

"Kom. I will speak with you."

We kind of slunk towards her. What else could we do? And all of a sudden I saw something even worse than her. Our things – all of them – our rucksacks, half empty, and all the stuff we'd unpacked, pyjamas and washing things and Kev's salty jeans, all heaped anyhow. And on top, my wet stuff, my pants and bra and T-shirts and socks, that I'd hung out on the balcony.

"You will leave," she said. That was all. One o'clock in the morning – out. Just like that.

I looked at Kev. He didn't have a word to say, so I had to say something. "Why? What've we done?"

"I will tell you. You are very bad young. You go together without married. That is your business and not mine. But when you speak so to my clerk because he is from Indonesia, and when you do hurt to him, that is my business. Also I do not allow that you suspend your underdressings in front of my hotel."

"What?"

"Your underdressings!" she shouted. She picked up my pants in one hand and my bra in the other and flapped them at me.

"That is not polite to expose to the street the underdressings! Such you may do in England but here we are more modest. Now you will take all dressings altogether and pay my bill and leave my hotel!"

Kev come-to smartish, when money was mentioned.

"We ain't paying," he said, "and that's flat! What you charging us for, throwing us out on the street in the middle of the night?"

"I charge you for dirt and laundry and for compensate my clerk! You will pay one night lodging or I call police."

We stood there. At last I nudged Kev. "You'd better pay," I said. I was thinking of the mud on the bedspread.

Kev fished out his wallet so slow you'd've thought it had weights on it. I felt like crying. I was ashamed and tired and scared.

"Where shall we go?" I asked in a choky voice.

Old Tyre-top looked at me, and her iron jaw softened a bit.

"How are you old?" she asked me.

"Sixteen. And three quarters," I added, like Lily, trying to feel older.

She unfolded her arms. Her big boobs sort of quivered.

"I give address," she said. She wrote something on a card and handed it to me. "Very cheap place, but clean. You take your cycle, reach there soon."

"Will they let us in, this time of night?" I was down on the floor stuffing the things into our rucksacks, still trying not to cry. I had to wipe my nose on my wet T-shirt.

"I telephone. They expect you."

Kev didn't say a thing. When he'd paid, he took the rucksacks from me and marched out. But if he thought he was shot of the whole business he was wrong, because just outside on the pavement was the clerk. The Indonesian. He was standing there with no expression on his face, holding our bikes ready for us.

Kev stopped dead and they looked at each other. Like a couple of dogs deciding whether to fight. I ran down the steps and grabbed my bike.

"Thanks for bringing them round," I said.

But he wasn't looking at me, only at Kev. He pushed his bike towards him. Kev didn't move.

"If you were half a man," said the clerk, "you would apologise to me."

"If you were half a man," Kev said, "I'd bash your face in."

I shut my eyes tight. Something inside me seemed to shut, too. I thought, *That's it. Not tonight. No matter what.* It's not enough to fancy someone. You've got to like him too. And I couldn't like Kev, not after that, not the same night anyway.

14 · Neils and Yohan

My great decision – not to have it away with Kev that night –
didn't count for much as it turned out. Because this place she
sent us to didn't have double bedrooms. They had sort of
dormitories instead. In fact it was a youth hostel, or something
like one. By the time we found it, and were let in, and registered,
and went out again to chain up our bikes, and dragged our junk
up the stairs, I could no more have got romantic than swum the
Channel. I was put in one room and Kev in another. There were
four beds in mine, three of them full of girls snoring. I pulled
my top clothes off and climbed into my sleeping-bag in my
"underdressings" and was asleep in two ticks.

Next day me and Kev met for breakfast in the canteen or
whatever you'd call it. I felt better. I always do in the mornings.
Every day's another day, after all. Whatever's happened the
night before, you can't go on being miserable forever. To be
honest there's very few things that don't strike my funnybone
after a good night's sleep. That fat lady waving my wet bra and
pants at me, and getting all uptight about me hanging them on
the balcony, that struck me as priceless. Specially after she'd let
us in in the the the first place, knowing we weren't married. Talk
about swallowing a camel and choking on a gnat!

But I agreed with her about her clerk; that wasn't on. The only
thing I couldn't have a bit of a private giggle over that morning
was Kev saying to that Indonesian that he wanted to bash his
face in.

Kev looked a bit hangdog. Perhaps he was ashamed, after all.
I hoped so. I decided that he was, and deserved cheering up.

"What we doing today?"

"I dunno. I've half a mind to go back to the others."

He'd half a mind? I'd a whole mind. I wanted to, more than
anything. It was babes-in-the-wood time, us here alone. But I
knew we'd never find them.

"We can't. We'll see 'em on Tuesday, on the boat, like you

said." This was Friday. We had three more days. . . . My heart sank a bit, I admit it. "We've got to try and keep out of trouble." I said.

"Yeah," said Kev, "and nightclubs. I'm thirty quid light after last night, bloody thieves!"

"We got our money's worth," I said. "At least, you got yours! Wasn't all that what you came here for in the first place? Dirtiest city in Europe, etcetera etcetera?"

He looked up at me, saw I was needling him, and grinned, sheepish. "Get away, that was nothing," he mumbled into his cheese roll. We were both eating like horses after our thin night.

"We got to face it, mate," I said, "all that steamy stuff's not for good little Catholics like us."

"You speak for yourself! Don't affect me."

"Course it does. Tell you the truth, when I looked at those two, stripped off and writhing about in that red spotlight, it was like a bit of hell."

"Bit of heaven, more like! I thought you wasn't looking at all."

"Peeped through my fingers once in a while, didn't I?"

"Well. At least you know now how it's done."

I burst out giggling. Couldn't help it.

"If old Cliff and Karen'd had a go at it like them two, that tent would've come apart!"

Kev choked into his coffee.

"Don't you worry, girl," he said, "you and me'll do it the good old-fashioned way."

I stopped giggling. I think I'd been kind of hoping he'd forget the whole idea. I couldn't face another three days of should I, shouldn't I.

"Listen, Kev. If you're short of cash, what's wrong with stopping here?"

He put his coffee cup down.

"Turn you off, did it, all that? The poufs, and them two going at it in public?"

"Well. A bit. Didn't it you?"

"No. The point of all that stuff is to turn you on."

"Oh," I said. I played about with my fork. There was a long silence. "Can I have seconds?" I asked finally.

"Trouble with you is, you can't get your mind off your

stomach."

"Yours is stuck even a bit lower down," I said, which I thought was rude, but quite good in its way. It shut him up about my appetite, anyway. And his, come to think of it.

*

Perhaps because of that, we had a nice day. Just sightseeing and that. We left the bikes behind and walked, and took trams. Darryl had said you had to travel like the "real people" did, to get to know a foreign town, and I saw his point. Being jammed in with hundreds of Amsterdamians (Kev called them "the Amsterdamned") in a tram, well, that's one way to get to know them. They're very polite, not much pushing, and they're nice and clean. Modest, too. I looked up at pretty near every balcony we passed to see if there were any underdressings suspended there. I'd hoped there would be, just one or two, but no. *Solid* against underdressings, the Dutch. I began to think I'd have felt more at home in Italy or somewhere, with all those strings of washing right across the streets.

One thing was really nice. We were walking along and we heard fairground music. Right in the middle of the town. Now I'm bent for fairs. Can't resist them, never could. Just the sound of that tonkly steam-engine music turns me on and gets me running. I was off like a shot down a sidestreet, and suddenly there we were in a big pedestrian precinct. It was market day seemingly. Loads of people, and half of them were standing around this huge *thing*.

I don't know if I can describe it. It was a music-machine, obviously, kind of like a big box on wheels with all kinds of carving and figures sticking out of it. All painted fair-ground colours, with lots of gold and silver. The figures were in fancy dress (except for some cherubs), the men in white curly wigs and long socks and the women showing a lot of chest and with little satin slippers, I mean painted of course. And they moved. They were all playing instruments, bells mostly. It was a treat how they moved and how they worked. And of course the sound. I stood and stood, just watching it working, and listening. Kev got fed up in the end.

"Oh come on! What's grabbing you? So it's a big old musical box on wheels. Let's go."

"Kev, you know what? You could keep all the groups, the Clash and even Sting, if I could have a thing like this banging away outside my window."

He looked at me as if I'd flipped my lid.

"You can't even dance to it."

"I could, if no one was looking. It's magic."

"It ain't working any spells on me. I'm going."

"Just another minute—"

He wouldn't, though, and I had to leave. But in the afternoon, we saw another one, even nicer, and this one had a little man on it who turned his head and *rolled his eyes* every time he clashed his cymbals, and that got Kev a bit; he said he looked as if he was going to have a fit. So I was allowed to watch that one for maybe ten whole minutes.

When I came out of my trance and looked round, I thought he'd run out on me, but then I saw him. He was away across this square, talking to some fellows. They were all drinking beer outside a little place like a pub.

Kev caught my eye and I thought he'd beckon me over, but instead he made a sign that I should stop where I was and look some more at the music-machine. Being me, of course, I didn't want to then. I wanted to see what he was up to. So I strolled across.

Kev didn't look too pleased, but he said, "This is Neils and this is – what you say your name was?"

"Yohan," said the other one. They were both Dutch, a lot older than us. Neils was tall and had short mousy hair like Cliff, and a little moustache. Yohan was short and darker, with a beard. He wore dark glasses. They were dressed a bit like Mods, long jackets and that. It struck me they were a bit old for that lark. I go for cults and fancy gear and that myself, but it always upsets me a bit when older people do it.

So these two blokes offered me a beer, which I took, and we sat down and talked about the weather. It had been exceptional, day after day of sun like that, but I didn't want to talk about it. I asked them what they did for a living, and Yohan grinned and said, "As little as we can." Their English was very good. "Are you out of work?" I asked. "In a way," they said. "Do you get social security? Or what?" I asked. Kev gave me a kick in the ankle. "What's wrong with asking that?" I said, narked, and he said, "None of your business, Nosy," which was true I suppose, so I shut up.

They seemed very maty, so we told them about getting kicked out of the Parkstaad Hotel. They thought it was a riot. When they finished killing themselves about my underdressings, they said, "And where do you stay now?" We told them the name of it and they looked at each other, and then Neils, the tall fair one, said, "That is not fun. Perhaps you like to stay with us."

"You got a place?"

"Yes," they said, "what you call a pad. Not very elegant, but there you are free to do as you like." They gave us a look, from Kev to me. I looked away across the square to the music-machine so they wouldn't see me blushing. I'd begun to wish we hadn't run into them.

"Maybe we'd best stop where we are," I said. "Thanks all the same."

But Kev had seen a way to save money.

"How much do you charge?" he asked, straight out. And when they both laughed and shook their heads, I saw Kev was in favour, a hundred per cent.

"Okay then," he said, before I could interrupt. "We'll fetch our gear and bikes. How shall we find you?"

The blokes said they'd come with us and give a hand. We were completely lost by then so it was a help, and what made me think again about our luck, meeting them, was that they took us most of the way by a boat with a glass roof and wouldn't even let us pay our own fares.

They gave us a sort of running commentary as we went along, pointing out places of interest and probably having us on a bit with their stories. I felt they were laughing at us behind our backs, though they kept straight faces when it showed. I wondered why they were bothering to be nice to us. What Sean had said about foreigners did cross my mind. But when we'd got our bikes and the rest of our stuff from the hostel, and walked with them half across the city to their house, I was too knackered to worry. We'd been on our feet the whole day and even if they'd lived in a doss-house I couldn't have moved another step.

And it wasn't a doss-house, not by a long chalk. Their flat was high up in one of the tall, narrow old houses, with stairs so steep we had to practically crawl up them. But when we got up, it wasn't half bad. You could see they did themselves all right, and why they weren't bothered about a few guilders for our rent. The main room went right from the front of the house to the back, under the sloping roof. It had a skylight and it was all very modern. The furniture was mostly black leather and chrome and glass, and the rugs were shag-pile in very bright colours to show up against all the wood and metal and plain dark walls. At the far end the wall was black, with no pictures, though there were pictures everywhere else – big glossy coloured photos like you see on calendars in workshops and in some other places – girls without much on in all sorts of sexy poses.

There was plenty of stereo equipment, and a big telly, and a lot of fancy lighting. Down at the end, where the black wall was, there were some stand-up photo-floods like they have in photographers' studios, and things which I only glanced at at first – one of them looked like a motorbike, of all things, under a dust-sheet. And there was a very expensive-looking camera on a tripod.

I moved round the room, looking at the photos.

"Is this what you do?" I asked. "Take photos for calendars?"

They laughed and said that was one thing they did, and did I want to look at some more of their art-work? Frankly I thought there was as much of it as I'd want to see stuck on the walls, so I said, "Okay, only later," and asked for the ladies'.

They showed me where it was. I got a start when I went in. It must have had about a two hundred watt bulb in there. The walls were all papered like a jungle and the toilet fitting was like an alligator's head – you had to open up its jaws to sit down. Luckily it didn't actually have teeth. . . .

When I turned to face the door I got another shock. There was a mask on it – carved and painted like a witch-doctor's mask – one of those very scary ones. Kind of leering at me. Something gleamed in the eye-holes. Something made me lift it off its nail, and then I saw that in the door, behind where the mask's eye-holes were, there were two little spy-holes with magnifying glass in, like you get in some ordinary front doors.

I couldn't believe it. I just stood there. Then I threw the door open. Nobody. . . . I went out and closed the door, leaving that bright light on, and peeped through a spy-hole.

That was when I should have left. I know that now. Why didn't I? Don't ask me. Con would have, and said a few choice words before she went, and all. But I didn't have the guts. So I just went back into the big room and sat down as if nothing had happened.

They'd poured out drinks, short ones. They gave me one. It was thick yellow stuff like custard, and I felt so shaky I drank it. They were all getting on like a house on fire, and I was left out, so I asked if I could put on some music. They showed me how the stereo worked – it was at the far side of the room from where they were all sitting drinking – and left me to it. I found a cassette of a Dutch group and put it on, and then I sat in a deep leather chair and put my feet up on a matching footrest. I sipped the yellow drink and listened to the music and after a bit I just sort of dozed off.

When I woke up it was dark. And I was on my own. They'd left one light on, right down the far end, and the stars were shining down through the skylight. The room had a funny smell in it – they must've been smoking like mad while I was asleep. I wondered what time it was, and then I saw the lit-up numbers in the digital radio-clock: *22.46*. Getting on for eleven at night! Mother of God! I must've just flaked out.

But where were they? Where was Kev?

I got up and turned on some more lights, and then I saw his note. It was on the black-topped coffee table among the ashtrays and sticky glasses and bottles. In his awful writing, it said:

Neils and Yohan wanted to take us out to a nightclub they know which is even worse than what we saw last night. I knew you wouldn't want to come and you was sleeping so we decided to nip off. Neils says there's food in the fridge, to help yourself. If you want to turn in, just use your sleeping-bag on the settee.

Kev

P.S. You want to try some of the liquoures, we left them all out for you. Try the green one, it's peppermint, got a kick like a kangeroo.

I stood there, staring at it, reading it over and over. It wasn't possible, but it was true. You'd think I'd have got it from that, wouldn't you? And simply never spoken to him again.

15 · Nasties in the Cupboard

I was so blazing mad, I hardly even bothered to look in the fridge. It was full of cheeses and lovely things like ham and fancy ice-cream. But I was too choked up to eat. I stamped back into the big room, read Kev's note again, started crying out loud, stopped because there was no point, and then looked at the bottles.

There were lots of them, all different shapes and with pretty-coloured drink in them. There was the thick yellow stuff, and the green, and some that looked like meths. A lot of the labels said *BOLS* so I shouted *"BOLS BOLS BOLS"* at the top of my voice. Then I got a big glass and poured a bit in from every bottle.

It didn't all mix. I switched on one of the strong photo-lamps at the back end of the room and held up the glass against it. The layers lay like a rainbow. It was so pretty it seemed a shame to tip it up and drink it. But I managed.

Strong? I'll say! Made me feel funny. Much funnier than those gins that time. I wanted to dance, so I put the cassette on again. I whirled around a bit on my own, but the room started whirling too so I kind of sat down on the floor. The Dutch singer was good. I shut my eyes and tried to think I was at home, listening to Sting, but he didn't sound anything like him really. I started to cry again.

Fancy Kev walking out on me like that. Just to see some horrible tarts taking their clothes off. I didn't know how he *could* want to see them when he could've been with me. Maybe that was the trouble. Maybe he was fed up with me because he wasn't getting what he wanted. Maybe he was so highly sexed he couldn't manage without. Maybe after he'd seen those sexy floor-shows he'd get so turned-on he'd go to some streets Neils had told us about on the boat, where the girls sit in their windows. *If* too much he was telling the truth. . . . He'd said if a man fancied them he just rung their doorbells and they'd let him in and have it off with him. Just like that.

It made me *sick*. The whole business made me sick. Why's it so different for men? Karen says it isn't, that girls are just the same really. But I don't believe it. How could a woman want it off with a man she'd never seen before? You've got to like the person, haven't you? Karen should talk. Cliff probably just did one wrong thing, or said one, and *chop!* She's so off him she won't talk to him. As for me, I couldn't even kiss a fellow I didn't like.

Did I like Kev?

The question flashed into my mind. I threw it out. If I didn't like him, I couldn't want him. So I must like him.

Did I want him?

Oh sod this drink! I thought drink was meant to *stop* you thinking, not make all sorts of thoughts and questions come into your head, all clear and sharp like the shadows from that bright photo-lamp. It was still shining away, onto the black wall and all the weird stuff they'd got down there. I thought I'd best turn it off. Must use an awful lot of electricity – Mum's always on at us to turn lights off.

I staggered down the room. The studio part on the other side of the light was quite hot. I looked at the stuff. I lifted the cover off the thing that looked like a motorbike and found it was a motorbike, brand new, painted red. I looked at some of the clothes on a clothes rack. Some of them were normal, but some of them were weird. For instance, there was a pair of jeans with a hole cut out of the back, like a key-hole. And there was a purple silky dress with borders of furry stuff, ever so soft. I held it up against me and pulled it this way and that, but I didn't see how you could wear it by itself, the neckline was down round the waist somewhere. I supposed they were what the calendar girls wore for photos.

Then I noticed a door in the wall, and opened it. More cameras were in there. And there were other things. Chains, hanging on hooks. Weird-looking bits of leather and rubber and stuff. Some were made into bits of clothes, but others – well, I couldn't make out what they were. Then, stacked against the back wall, I saw a pile of boxes. I opened the top one and looked in. And closed it again, quick.

What kind of photos did those boys take, anyway? I came out of there in a hurry. Suddenly that end of the room with its black wall and its hot, glaring light was somewhere to get far away from.

I wished Kev was here. No I didn't. I wished Dad and Vlady were here, or if not, Con or Michael. I had an idea if Michael saw all that stuff in the cupboard he'd have me out of that flat in two minutes. I wished I could go. That'd pay Kev out, if he came back all – all cocksure, and found me gone. I started giggling at the idea. I finished my drink. I'd heard they invent fancy names for cocktails, so I decided to call mine Tracy's Multicoloured Gobstop. I must've been pretty well away by then because I picked up the phone, which was on the floor, and said:

"Hallo, is that Noel Edmonds? Tracy Just here. I'd like to swop a box of whips and some sexy gear for a bike with wings to fly me back to the youth hostel in Rotterdam."

Through the buzzing in my ear, I distinctly heard Noel say he'd got one, to come down the steep stairs backwards and I'd find it waiting for me outside.

*

The buzzing was still going on when I woke up next. I jerked myself up. I was all stiff and sore from lying on the floor. The phone was off the hook so I put it back. And that awful lamp was still glaring away. And Kev still wasn't back, though the digital clock said *02.46*.

The youth hostel in Rotterdam.

I'd been dreaming about it, over and over again, me trying to get there, running to get there. Suddenly I thought, *Maybe they haven't left, maybe they're all still there!* Would it have a phone? Yes it would!

Something in my head said to me very clearly, "You're going to have to think, and you're boozed. Get unboozed." I climbed carefully to my feet and took short steps into the kitchen. Actually I didn't feel too funny any more, but the buzzing was still in my ear from the phone and my eyes were sparkling round the edges. I opened the fridge again and took out a hunk of ham and some of that Dutch cheese with red wax round it. I plugged in the electric kettle. I knew from Sean that coffee's good for deboozing so I looked for some. There was no instant, but I found some real coffee. Do you know, I'd never tasted it? I only recognised it because I'd smelt it, passing the coffee-shop in Ealing. No clue how to make it properly, but I just bunged some in a mug and poured the boiling water on and it worked – sort of. Tasted dead bitter, but I treated it like medicine and drunk it all and by the last swallow I was liking it. Ate the cheese and ham, and some rolls I found, and then I got out the carton of fancy ice-cream (maple and walnut, I think it was) and tucked in with a big spoon. By the time I'd had enough, it was gone and the sparkling and buzzing had too.

Now to find a phone book. I went back into the big room, and right away I saw one, on one of the shelves. I grabbed it – but of course it had to be the Amsterdam one.

Now then, I thought, *Trace, you got to be dead clever.* How would a Dutch person look up a number in London, I mean like in Brum if he was in London? He'd phone Directory Enquiry. Did they have it in Holland? Of course they did. And where could you look, to find Directory's number? Front of the phone book, right? I turned to the front of the phone book.

Loads of words. Loads of numbers. All Dutch to me.

I felt desperate. But then I thought, *Some words in Dutch aren't so different.* Maybe the word "enquiry" is a bit like our word. So I ran my finger down the list. Nothing like enquiry. But there was just one word beginning with "en" – *enlichtian.* Enlighten? Worth a try.

I dialled. It rang. Maybe they shut down at night? My heart was going – I don't know what'd got into me – I just had to try, and I had to do it now. A voice answered in Dutch.

"Please," I said, "can you speak English?"

"Yes?"

"Is that Directory Enquiry?"

"Yes."

Oh thank you, Holy Mother! (I only turn to Her in really desperate moments of course.)

"I need a number. In Rotterdam."

"What is the name, please?"

"It's a youth hostel."

"Which one?"

"The Rotterdam one!"

"In Rotterdam are several youth hostels."

Oh no. But wait! I had my map that Michael gave me, with the right hostel circled.

"Please! Wait a minute!"

I rushed at my rucksack and burrowed in it, tossing everything on the floor. Then I remembered it was in one of the side pockets and found it right away. I tore it, unfolding it too quick. There was Michael's circle. I grabbed the phone and gabbled out the name of the street from the map.

"Just a minute please."

It was a pretty Polish minute, which means it was more like five hours. But finally she came back. She'd got it!

"Thanks a lot! Thank you!" I yelled down the phone.

Then I dialled the number.

The phone rang a long time. Well, it would – three in the morning. I was thinking to myself, *You must be losing your marbles, they'll never answer*, when someone did.

"Ve is dar?" (or something) said a very angry, sleepy voice.

"Do you speak English?"

"Yes, god-damn it," said the voice. I could hear now he was American. "But I don't like speaking it or any other god-damned language in the middle of the night! Waddaya want?"

"I want to know if Michael Driscoll's there."

"Who the hell is he?"

"Excuse me, do you run the hostel?"

"No. I just try to get some sleep here but the god-damn phone's just outside my room."

"I'm sorry," I said. My voice must have wobbled, because he said, in a nicer way, "Is it an emergency? You sound a bit—"

"I just want to speak to Michael Driscoll," I said. "But he's probably left."

"Has he got two heads or anything, so I might have noticed him around?"

"He's only got one head. It's red. And he's got some teenagers with him. Two boys and two girls."

"Oh, him! Yeah, I think I saw him at breakfast time. I don't know if they're still around. . . . Couldn't you phone in the morning? Like, the proper morning, say seven a.m?"

I didn't answer. I couldn't. I couldn't imagine coping until seven a.m. I wanted Michael now.

"Hey! Are you still there?"

"Yeah," I said, gulping.

"Are you crying or something? I can hardly hear you."

"I'm okay."

"No you're not. Hang on. I'm going to see if I can locate a red head sticking out of its sleeping-bag."

There was a long, long pause. I sat on the leather chair and sniffed. I hadn't much hope. That was why it was so wonderful when I heard Michael's voice on the other end.

"Tracy?"

"Michael?"

"Tracy, are you all right?"

"No."

"What do you mean? You in some sort of trouble?"

"Not exactly. . . . Michael, I'm coming back to Rotterdam."

"We're leaving tomorrow."

"Please don't go till I come back! I'll catch the first train! Couldn't you meet me at the station?"

"Where's Kev?"

"He's gone to a nightclub."

"Are you all alone?"

"Yeah."

There was a silence. Then he said, "Where are you?"

"In a flat. Of some boys we met."

"Are you scared or what?"

I thought about that. "I think I'm just dead lonely."

"I could kill him," said Michael.

"Me too," I said.

"How could he leave you?"

"I dunno, do I."

"Whose flat did you say you were in?"

"Two fellows. Dutch."

"Are they okay?"

I glanced at the black wall and the cupboard, and I thought of the toilet. "I don't kow."

"What you mean?"

"They take photos. For calendars and that."

"You mean, girls?"

"Yeah."

"Well, that's not so bad. Anything happen you don't like?"

"No. . . . But I found something. Some *things*."

"Like what?"

I swallowed. I felt silly saying it. "Whips."

"What?"

"Whips. In a box. In a cupboard."

There was a silence.

"And there's some other funny stuff in there too," I added, in case he should think I was being stupid.

"Tracy, have you got a lamp on your bike?"

My heart near stopped. Did he think it was that bad?

"I'm not riding to Rotterdam in the night, if that's what you're thinking!" I said.

"No," he said. "No, perhaps that's— Listen though, Tracy. I don't like the sound of it. But Kev's there – I mean, he will be. You get in your sleeping-bag now and go to sleep. Don't let 'em get you up, I mean if they come home and say they want to have a party or anything like that, just pretend to be asleep and don't get up. Then in the morning, you – and Kev if he'll come, but never mind if he won't, you come anyway – ride to the railway station and get on the first train like you said. Try and get one about six. I'll meet every train till you get here. Got it?"

"Yeah, I got it."

"Now don't worry. And don't – er – don't undress. Get in your sleeping-bag the way you are. Okay?"

"Yeah. Michael—"

"What?"

"I'm sorry for what I said."

"When?"

"Before we went off."

"Forget it. I have."

I didn't want to hang up and lose his voice, but what else was there to say?

"I'm going now," I said. "'Night."

"'Night, Tracy."

There was a long pause. I waited for him to hang up first. But he didn't. Finally I said, "Michael?"

"Yeah?"

"What you still there for?"

"Waiting for you to hang up."

"Let's hang up together. Ready steady, go."

But still we didn't. So there was another long pause, and then I heard them, a long way down, coming up the steep narrow stairs.

"Michael! They're coming!"

"Oh Christ!" He just breathed it. "Tracy – do what I told you – it's all right – they're just porn-merchants, they're not dangerous – I wish I was there—"

And suddenly I felt brave. I was able to say, "It's okay, I can take care of myself." My voice sounded like Con's. I was thinking of her when I said it. She'd see anyone in hell before she'd let them mess about with her. "Don't worry. See you tomorrow." And I hung up, grabbed my sleeping-bag from the floor, and dashed through a door up my end of the room.

It was their bedroom of course. It had a key in the lock and I turned it. Sleep on the settee, indeed! Sod *that* for a lark. Let them sleep on the settee, all the lot of them. I unrolled my bag with one good flick, flung it on one of the beds, kicked off my trainers and wriggled in like a galloping caterpillar.

Next door I heard them all come in. Kev was talking loud. Being one of the lads. They were all full of booze and fooling about, but then they must've looked round for me, and they went quiet.

"Trace? Trace, where are you?"

I lay curled up in my bag. Someone tried the door handle.

"She's locked herself in," Kev said.

"I think you tell her to sleep in here," said one of them.

"I did!"

"That is our bedroom. She can't sleep there."

Oh can't I? I thought. *Try stopping me!*

A loud knocking. I curled up tighter and put my fingers in my ears.

"Trace – let me in!"

Oh, sure.

"*Please*, Trace— "

Push off to another porn show, see what that does for you. I'm stopping here. I felt like shouting it aloud, but I didn't. Michael had told me to pretend to be asleep, and even though they couldn't get at me, I still somehow did what he told me.

"Tracy— " Now it was one of the others; Neils, I think. "Wake up! We are going to have a nice party!"

Ha! Very nice, I'm sure. And next thing you know, you'll be asking me to put on those key-hole jeans and get chained up to that motor-bike and get my photo taken. I know your game.

They tried a few more dodges to get a rise out of me, but in the end they gave up. There wasn't any party, either. They just grumbled and mumbled a bit and then everything went quiet. I had a lovely picture in my mind of them all dossing down on the floor before I dropped off to sleep.

16 · Reunion

In spite of my late night I was awake next morning at the crack. I tiptoed to the door, opened it and peeped out. Sure enough, there they all were, the rotten swine, snoring away in heaps of rugs and stuff all over the place. They hadn't given Kev the settee, I noticed.

My gear was still spread around a bit and I had to be dead cautious. I crept in like a shadow and picked it all up. Then I took it back in the bedroom and packed, and rolled up my bedding. I wanted to have a wash and there was a basin in there but I was afraid to make any noise, so I just wiped my face on my wet T-shirt again and sneaked out.

Down the steep dark stairs – backwards round the corners, my pack made me feel someone was pushing me down a mountain – and out into the morning. The pouring wet morning. Yeah, the fine weather had broken, wouldn't you know? Never mind. I fished out my cagoule and stuck it on and hoped my rucksack was as waterproof as Sean had said. One glance up at the house and I was off.

The cobbles were slippery and I was glad to get on a cycle track and start whizzing along to the station. There wasn't much traffic and I suddenly realised it was Sunday. I wondered what it'd be like to go to church in Holland. . . . I wouldn't have minded, I felt I needed a bit of holy water – pity you can't take your brain out and give it a wash, get rid of some of the muck. Still, the rain'd have to do the job.

I don't like rain, but I liked it that morning. It wasn't cold, it just streamed down, washing my face and hands for me and bringing up the curl in my hair, what there is of it. I couldn't help thinking, *If I get to Rotterdam looking half-drowned, Michael'll feel sorry for me and not be too mad at me.*

I was on the platform waiting for the Rotterdam train before I thought about Kev at all. I'd been so fed up with him that I'd sort of lumped him together with the two Dutchmen. But now, standing there on my own, I thought of him waking up, with a head like a rotten cabbage, and finding I'd flown the coop. What would he feel like?

At first I giggled to myself, thinking of it. But after a bit I began thinking he might worry, and that perhaps I ought at least to've left him a note. Even when he was running out on me last night, he'd done that much. Maybe I ought to go back?

I couldn't. I didn't know the way. I'd found the station okay just by getting on a main road and then looking at my map, but go back again I couldn't, all those twisty little streets. . . .

The train came in. I loaded my bike on, and then found a seat, and we were off. The sun had come out now and all the fields were shining. It was a pity we were too late to see the bulbs blooming; it was just rows and rows of green leaves now. I liked watching them though, opening like a fan as we flashed past, a fan with its top towards you. Must be lovely in spring, all the daffs and tulips. And the hyacinths. Mum's favourite flower, hyacinths. God! I remembered – hadn't sent off my postcards, and we were going home in two days! Not worth it now. Shame.

A man came along the train with lovely fresh rolls with ham and that cheese full of holes. I bought two, but my eyes were bigger than my stomach. I'd gone mad for that Dutch cheese. Beats old mousetrap every time.

I was getting excited now. And nervous. What'd Michael say to me? He'd seemed nice enough on the phone last night but I'd caught him on the hop – he'd have had time to think now, remember what I'd said to him and that. I'd know – soon as I saw him – if he was going to tell me off or sulk with me. I thought of what he'd said to Kev, about hating idiots like him. I didn't know what I felt about that now. All I knew was, if he said anything like that to me, I'd curl up and die.

We got there. It was still early – about eight o'clock – but I never had a doubt Michael'd be there, and sure enough, there he was. Good to see him? I'll say. There's a lot to be said for older men. They're bigger, for one thing. Michael looked dead solid, standing there. I had a funny moment when I nearly dropped my bike and ran into his arms. Except his arms weren't held out, so I didn't, of course.

"So there you are," he said, not committing himself.

135

"Yeah, here I am."

"Where's Kev?"

"Still snoring I expect."

"Tell him you was going?"

"No," I said. "Why should I?" – though as I said before, I knew I should have.

He thought for a sec, then said, "Well, it's too late now. Come on, the others are waiting at the hostel. We're going to try to make Madurodam today."

"What, that miniature town?"

"Yeah."

"Did you go up the Euromast tower yet?"

"Day before yesterday."

"Was it good?"

"Great. See for miles. And they got this spiral lift, goes up like a corkscrew so you get a view all round."

We were biking along, side by side. I was thinking. Was I glad or sorry I'd gone with Kev, now it was over?

"Well, I've seen Amsterdam, anyhow," I said.

"Yeah. Backside of it and all," he said, without knowing the half of it.

It was great to see the others again. They were all in the dining-room of the hostel, eating a big breakfast. They gave me a kind of sarcastic cheer as I came into the room. Darryl said, "The prodigal returns!" and Con gave me one of her sideways grins. Karen and Cliff were sitting together. On a bench, close. Looked like they'd made it up. I sat next to Con.

"How'd you get on?" she asked.

"Okay," I said. "Well. In a way. Miss me?"

"Been too busy. We done loads of things. What've you done? Anything I wouldn't?"

I got red of course. "Tell you later."

Turned out it was our group's turn to wash up for the whole bloody hostel. Talk about turning up in the nick of time! Con and me washed, and Karen and Cliff dried. Practically close enough to use the same cloth.

"They're all turned on again I see," I whispered to Con.

"Nothing doing while we're sleeping here of course, it's convent-and-monastery time. But give 'em a two-man tent and you won't see 'em for dust."

We were scrubbing out last night's pots. "Fancy you doing a bunk like that," she said. "Michael wasn't half upset."

"Yeah? How d'you know?"

"How'd you think? He didn't hide it, he was running round in circles."

I tried not to show how I felt about that. Easy really, seeing I wasn't sure myself, but I felt *something*.

"I see you and Darryl stuck with the group. No dossing down in haystacks."

"Yeah, well, *we* couldn't very well go when Michael was all panic-stations about you and Kev. He'd've gone off his trolley altogether, worrying."

"D'you mind?"

"No, it's been okay. We had a lovely meal last night in a proper restaurant, with a floorshow."

I pricked up my ears. "Yeah? What kind?"

"Acts and that. Ventriloquist. A singer – South American. And some sort of Eastern dancers, fantastic. Cost us a bomb, but it was worth it. Michael made us all clean up, even had to iron our tops. As it was he had a job getting us in because we weren't dressed up enough. Michael's got a way with him, I'll say that. Remember how he got round that camp-site commandant to let us have a fire? If I didn't know him better I'd say he gives 'em back-handers. But I think it's just his fatal Irish charm."

We finished the dishes at long last and the others settled up. Darryl showed me the leaflets about Madurodam. Looked great. It was near the Hague, another big town, but it wasn't all that far. The others said they were getting in such good shape from all the cycling, they could do sixty miles a day and still be ready to go out in the evening – they'd done it the day before. Been to a cheese market, hadn't they, and gobbled cheese till they nearly burst. Bought some fancy candles for their mums, at least Karen and Darryl had. Seen about a million windmills and even been in to one. It's true Michael had made them go through a museum and look at some boring old stuff, but even there they saw a gold goblet which was meant to be the best in the world, which might have been okay.

Still. I told them about the musical boxes on wheels, and our

137

boat-ride on the canals. And I told them I'd been to two nightclubs with fabulous floorshows, without going into details. I thought Michael looked at me a bit sideways but he didn't ask anything.

We were on the road by nine-thirty. The weather was nice now, a bit blowy on the green open bits but then you'd expect that. I was fine to start with, zooming along with the others ; but after a bit I started falling behind. Got a bit of a headache, as well as leg-ache. Trouble was, the others had been riding every day and I hadn't. Not to mention Tracy's Multicoloured Gobstop, which seemed to be catching up with me a bit behindtimes. Before we'd got near the Hague they were having to wait for me.

"What's up with you then?" Michael said. "Been living it up too much, eh?"

"Looks like it," I said. "Seems hard to pedal somehow."

Michael inspected my tyres. "No wonder," he said. "Looks like you got a slow puncture. You better pump it up for now and we'll try and mend it when we get there."

That was when I found out my pump had gone missing.

"How'd you manage that?" asked Michael.

"Dunno. Must've been nicked in Amsterdam."

He pumped up my tyre for me, which I could've done for myself. Karen stood there with her eyebrows in the air, looking at me over Michael's back as he bent down pumping. Got me narked, so I said, "What you smirking like that for?"

"Just we were getting a lecture yesterday. Weren't we, Michael, eh?"

Michael grunted.

"About how if women want equal rights they can't expect men to spoil 'em no more, doing little things for 'em as if they was incapable. Eh, Michael? Is poor old Tracy incapable, Michael, eh, Michael?"

Cliff laughed, a great hoot, and even Con smiled. But Darryl said, "Shut up, he's just pumping her tyre, that's all! I done Con's yesterday and come to that, who mended *your* chain for you last night?"

That shut Cliff up, but not Karen. She said, "Yeah, but he wasn't sounding off about women's lib, was he? So get stuffed."

138

We rode on in not such a good mood as before.

Still, it all blew away soon enough. It was good, being back on the road with the others, though it felt funny without Kev. Con came alongside me and seemed to read my thoughts.

"Where'd you ditch Kev then?"

"Amsterdam."

"That's not very nice."

"Nice! If you want to know, he run out on me last night." And I told her about it.

"What a rotten sod," she said. "Pity you didn't push him in a canal."

We rode along for a bit, looking at the fields. Then she said, "You want to tell me?"

"What?"

"You know."

"Nothing happened," I said. I told her how we'd spent those two nights, getting kicked out of the hotel and that.

"Poor Trace," she said. Nice. The way she understood and didn't laugh.

17 · After the Little Town

Maybe one day I'll be a travel writer. If I ever get my spelling right. If I am, I'll start with a whole book about Madurodam.

This isn't it, though, so I must keep it short. But it's a smashing place. I always was mad for miniature things. I never had a dolls' house but Lily's got one, and if you want to know, Mary and me played with it more than Lil ever did; in fact we used to give her hell if she came along and mucked up our arrangements. Hours we spent, doing the rooms, putting up new wall-paper and that, and we never, not for years, gave poor Lily anything for Christmas or birthdays except miniature furniture and stuff for *us* to play with. She got so fed up one year, *she* give *us* each a set of dolls' furniture from Woolies. Mary was sixteen by then and she wasn't half livid. Lily said, "Serve you right, now you can start giving me stuff for my Sindy doll."

So It was Mary I was missing more than Kev as I wandered round this fantastic little town. There was a whole small park-full of it. You couldn't even see it all at once unless you climbed up the banks that were round it. It was just like a real town, with everything in it – even smoke coming out of some of the chimneys. And things moved. You could put coins into little slots (or wait till someone else did) and see town bands playing and choirs marching into cathedrals, with lights shining through the stained-glass windows and real singing from inside. There were harbours with boats and ships coming and going, and one of them – that was what Darryl liked best – *on fire*; I mean real flames, with the little toy firemen playing a hose with real water to put it out. Then after a bit it'd start burning again.

Of course after that it was no surprise to see cars dashing along the roads and a cable-car going up a mountain and planes moving along runways and a fair (that was my favourite) with the ferris wheel going round. Some of the buildings were amazing. Just amazing. So real! Town halls and blocks of offices and little rows of houses and shops, and castles and palaces and churches – you name it, they had it, the tallest of them not higher than your waist.

I could've stopped there all day, or what was left of it, but Michael wasn't having any. We'd only one more day left, and he was getting jumpy– he hadn't seen a half nor a quarter of what it had in his guide-book. So after about two hours he dragged us away.

Him and Darryl wanted to go to the Hague – "After all, it is the capital". But the rest of us were knackered and wanted a rest. The sky was clouding over again, and Michael said we'd be better off indoors, but we knew what that meant – some museum or public building where he could get stuck in his book or gape at the architecture and we could go bananas.

So we split up, after arranging where to meet – we were camping that night by the sea. Michael and Darryl took off for the city while we pointed ourselves at the coast, and pretty soon we came to a seaside town called Swimagain, or something like that. It was pretty much like Brighton, except it had a sandy beach, but that was okay by us; we were ready for a few souvenir shops and cafés and that, not to mention a smashing pier with four sprouts on legs at the far end – and a tower.

"I'm going up that," I said, straight off. I love towers, and I'd missed the Euromast. But Karen and Cliff wanted to eat and buy stuff, so Con and me trailed along, and after watching them for a bit it struck me I hadn't bought anything for the family yet, so I got stuck in to a bit of shopping too.

I got one of those little blue and white dishes for Mum, with a Dutch scene painted on it (yeah, with a windmill – well, after all, she'd expect it, wouldn't she?). For Mary I got a headscarf with Dutch girls all over it, and for Lily a little pair of clogs, just about right for her Sindy doll. The men were harder to choose things for, like always, but in the end I got a miniature bottle of that yellow custard stuff for Sean (it's called advocaat) and for Dad a box of liqueur chocolates and a Dutch cigar.

Vlady was the big problem. He doesn't smoke or drink. When I think of him I just think of books. So in the end I got him a tiny silver book with a hook fastening. When you opened it, a sort of concertina of little pictures of Holland dropped out.

Con followed me about but she didn't buy anything.

"Aren't you getting nothing for your family?" I asked her. Not that she's got much, there's only her and her mum and dad.

"I'll buy 'em a cheese just before we get on the boat," she said. "I got a real old-fashioned Dutch pipe for Grandad already."

"What about souvenirs?"

"What for? I won't forget. Besides, I got my diary."

"You been writing about us on the sly?" I asked her.

"I been keeping it for four years now."

"Get away," I said. "What sorts of things do you write?"

"Everything, pretty near."

"When do you do it? Must take hours."

"I got a kind of shorthand I made up myself. I don't write every day. When we was camping I couldn't, so I just made notes, and when we got to the Youth Hostel and I had a table and that, I wrote up three days at once."

"Can I read it?"

She gave a laugh. "When it's published."

"There'll be some red faces then, I bet! Am I in it?"

"Course you are. But your face won't be red, don't worry."

The others had disappeared – probably necking somewhere. It had come on to rain again. We chained up our bikes to one of the bike-stands they have everywhere, and walked out along the pier.

"Have you changed much since you started your diary?"

"Course. I wasn't a punk then, was I."

I looked at her. She hadn't put on make-up for nearly a week. Her face was tanned and her hair was all blown back and curly from the sea air. You could see the roots weren't black.

"You're not one now if you ask me."

"Yes I am, I'm a real one, not like Kev and Cliff. Or you."

"What you mean?"

"You lot don't know what punk's all about. It's protest, isn't it. But what've you lot got to protest about? Families that you like, homes that you want to stay in. Rules you don't mind sticking to. . . . Darryl, now, he'd make a good punk, maybe, if he could get the hang of it, with a lush for mother and no Dad. But he's no rebel, not Darryl. He copies Michael, and Michael's a conformer. He likes society, likes the way it's run, more or less; he's prepared to fit in. Get a job, work hard, save money, buy a house, raise a family, do it all better than your parents – that's his idea. But it's not mine."

"What's yours then?"

She shrugged. "I want to change things. I dunno how, yet. All I know is, I look around and I don't like what I see. People's either well-off and settled, and smug and shut in to themselves, not caring for anyone so long as they can keep what *they* got – or else they're down and miserable and got nothing to hope for and no chance of getting it if they had. Both ways is dead boring and rotten and I'm not going to get stuck with either of 'em. So me, I'm going to be different. Just now the way to be different is to dye your hair and wear a lot of kinky gear that makes the smug lot feel sick and maybe makes the sad sort sit up a bit and even have a laugh and think life's not so – I dunno, so *fixed* as they thought, not if people can dress up mad and swear on telly and shock people, and sing protest songs, and have punch-ups and break all the rules. . . . It don't hurt no one, but it stops some people thinking they know the score about everything. They like to know which pigeon-hole everybody's in, but they've had to make a new one for the punks. They'd've labelled it 'Rubbish' or 'the Dregs' if we hadn't give it a worse label first. So now we're in all the papers, so they got to think about us, they got to listen to our message. If only because we scare 'em shitless. Which is no more than most of 'em deserve, seeing they don't give a monkey's about anyone but themselves."

I never heard Con go on like that. I couldn't think of a thing to say. So I said, "Let's go up the tower."

So we went up the tower, all 140 feet of it, and stood at the top looking down at the harbour and the big ships and the little ships, and the huge hotels and the stone breakwaters, and the horizon lost in the rain.

At last I said, "Black's for violence."

"What?"

"That's what you said once. When I asked why you go for all black gear. You said 'Black's for violence'."

"That's right."

"But you're not for violence. When you were a prefect, you stopped fights and that. You was on the side of law and order in school."

143

She didn't say anything for a while, just looked out at the sea.

"I've had enough of this tower," she said suddenly. "And the pier. Let's go back to the beach. I might want to swim."

"Swim? In the rain?"

"It's lovely and warm in the rain."

"You're crazy."

"I know. Coming?"

Well, I wasn't in the mood to be on my own so I stuck with her and we walked back along the pier. Half-way, she started.

"Listen, Trace," she said. "I'm in a talking mood, so I'll tell you something, only keep it to yourself. Remember that night we went to the Music Mill. You was surprised, wasn't you, that Mum let me go. When you rung the doorbell that night I'd just been watching the start of a row between my mum and dad. Last time he went for her like that, she wound up at that place in Chiswick, that home for battered wives. That was two years ago. Dad talked her round and made promises and I got at her too, told her I was scared to be home alone with him, though he never laid a hand on me, but I wanted her back so bad I lied to her. So she come back and it's been like living on a volcano ever since. Sometimes it starts rumbling and I start sweating, thinking what happened that time, with me standing there watching, too shit-scared to do anything to help her. . . . So that night you come, the volcano was rumbling. They was starting on each other. And I couldn't stand it, I wanted out. And she wanted me out. She never liked me seeing it, she says me being there makes him worse. In the end nothing happened; I mean she had no marks on her next morning, so he must've held his temper. That time. But I've lived with violence. I know where it's at. That's why I jumped on it at school. I wear all that black gear because of other people's violence, not mine. You seen how they avoid me in the street. That's what I like. They're scared of me. They keep away. That way they'll never find out how scared I am of them."

I gave a shaky little laugh. I felt so sorry for her, I had to make light of it somehow. "Call yourself a punk!" I said.

"I'll fight my own way," she said. "Punch-ups and angry Rock and that's okay for some, it's one way. I got other ways."

"Maybe you'll write for the papers."

She gave me a surprised look.

"No," she said. "Just living my own way. Seeing how I can manage. Breaking rules, making new ones, to fit *me*. It's fun. Life's got to be fun, hasn't it? Or where's the sense? I don't live my life to please no one but me."

"Why didn't you do a bunk, then, leave Michael, like you said, and sleep in barns and that?"

"Didn't want to in the end, did I? I'd've gone if I'd wanted, but I didn't want to, so I stuck."

"Because of Darryl?"

"No. Darryl's okay, he's got more to him than I ever thought, but I don't really fancy him. I never really fancied a bloke yet, if you must know. I like girls more, so far."

"Don't tell me you're gay!" I joked.

"I might be. I wouldn't care. Nothing wrong with gays. People find what they're looking for. Trouble is, most of 'em don't bother looking, they just stand there and let it all wash over them. Me, I'm going to swim right out into the middle of it!"

And with that, she suddenly did one of her nutties. We were back on the prom now. She jumped down the steps onto the beach and started running towards the sea. As she ran, she tore her clothes off – she did – right down to her pants, and she ran straight into the water in the rain.

I stood there, gaping at her. There weren't many people about because of the weather, but the ones there were had a good look, you can bet – she's got a nice figure, Con has. Not that she gave them long to look. She just belly-dived straight into a wave and started swimming like mad in the direction of England, leaving a trail up the beach – bra, jeans, top, cagoule, shoes, rucksack – honest, she's crazy.

After I got over the surprise, I climbed down and just walked to the water's edge, picking up her things and stuffing them into her rucksack so they wouldn't get rained on. I had a stupid idea she really would just swim and swim and I'd never see her again, and to be honest it did seem like an hour before I saw her coming back.

The mad mood was off her and I saw she wasn't keen to come out topless, so I flung her T-shirt to her and she pulled it on under water. Then she stood up in the grey waves and walked

145

out with her shirt clinging to her, all goosebumps and with her nipples sticking out like Raquel Welch in that 007 film. I didn't know where to look. But a couple of Dutch boys who'd seen her go in, and been standing there waiting, they knew where to look all right.

She took no notice, of course. She just came up to me and took her things off me, unrolled her jeans, and pulled them on her wet legs. The rain was stopping, luckily. The sun suddenly popped out, low down near the horizon under the dark clouds, making a red path down the sea towards us and turning the sand golden. Con got out a towel and started rubbing her hair till it all stuck up on end. The Dutch boys were coming nearer from behind, ogling us – well, Con – and talking to each other out the sides of their mouths. I didn't think Con had noticed them, but when they were close enough to hear her without her speaking loud, she just said, in her best prefect's voice, "Piss off, you two," still rubbing her head and not looking round. They did.

"Come on," she said to me, cool as can be, "let's go and get some tea."

*

The weather came up a treat that evening. The camping site was right on the front and we made a fire again and had a proper party. When it got dark some of us went in swimming and there were a lot of dares, to go in in the raw and that, but it was moonlight so I didn't. I did take my bathing suit off in the water just to see how it felt, and it felt fantastic, all sort of soft, specially where you're usually covered. But I kept it in my hand and struggled into it again before I came out.

We finished up with a sing-song. Very romantic, sitting by the fire, all glowing from sea and back-to nature somehow. . . . I sat next to Michael. I didn't decide to, or put myself forward, it just happened. I was dressed again and feeling nice and warm, but I didn't say anything against him putting a rug round my shoulders and warning me about catching cold after my swim. Karen and Cliff only sat with the rest of us for a bit, then they sort of crept away into their tent. Con was by herself on the other side of the fire. Darryl was moving about, getting wood and that, and helping make some hot coffee. I pulled his jeans' leg as he went past.

"Why don't you go sit with Con? She's lonely," I whispered.
He looked across the fire at her, and hesitated.

"No she's not."

"How'd you know?"

"I know her by now. She'd rather be on her tod."

Pity, though. Darryl was getting nicer all the time. And he really fancied Con, you could see that with one eye shut.

I felt sleepy. It'd been a long day. The singing was kind of quiet and dreamy and I began to nod off. I felt my head bump against Michael's shoulder and I jerked up straight.

"It's okay if you want to lean," he said. And I did want to, just to see what a really broad shoulder felt like. But I was too shy, somehow.

"Sorry I'm not Kev," he said, teasing.

"I'm not," I said before I'd thought. No "Should I, shouldn't I" tonight anyway. I wondered whether I was missing him, and decided I wasn't, but I told myself it was because I was too sleepy. It was great, just sitting there under the stars, listening to the singing and letting the sand run through my fingers.

There was no talking in bed that night. I was asleep before I'd crawled all the way into the tent. I never even heard Con come in. Had a few funny dreams though, all about hunting for my bicycle pump, riding about Amsterdam peering into the gutters saying, "I must find it, I must find it!" In the end Michael rode towards me holding it up in front of him saying, "I'll give it to you!" And Kev came out of nowhere and knocked him flying and shouted, "Let me give it to her, or I'll bash your face in." Well, maybe I've added a bit to make it sound good, but I know it was something like that.

Next day was our last day. We had a meeting in the morning, after breakfast, to decide what to do.

Karen and Cliff wanted to just lie about on the beach and spend the rest of their money on some nice grub – they hadn't much left anyway. Darryl surprised us all by announcing that he wanted to go to some bird sanctuary. Of all things!

"You can go by boat," he said. "It's on an island. There's thousands of different birds there, all in their proper habitats."

"What kind of birds?" Cliff mocked him, and I started singing, *"On Ilkley Moor Bah t'habitat—"* But Con said, "How far is it?"

147

Darryl looked at her. He had a gleam of hope in his eye. "Not far," he said. "And the boat goes to other lakes and that, it's a whole day's trip." He kept looking at her.

"Well," she said, "it might be okay. Do they have hot-houses for the tropical ones? Like in the zoo?"

"Yeah!" Darryl said, all eager now. "And things like ice-caves for the Arctic ones, and there's ostriches strolling on the lawns!"

I began to think I might like to go myself, but when Con gave one of her shrugs and said, "Yeah, okay, I'll go," I took one look at Darryl's face and I knew I couldn't. Not that he had a hope; I knew that now after what she'd said, but he'd never forgive me if I was there to stop him having a go.

So that left me and Michael. I looked at him and my heart sank a bit.

"I suppose you're going to museums and that again," I said.

"Not today," he said. "Sun's shining, I want to be outdoors."

"Shall we stop here then?" – only I didn't want to, not with Karen and Cliff carrying on like love-sick poodles.

"We could make a trip too, if you like," he said.

"Where to?"

The old guide-book was out in two ticks of course.

"Well," he said, "there's a little place near Gouda where we might have some fun."

I looked round at the others, expecting them to set up a howl at the word "fun", but Karen and Cliff were wandering down to the beach with their arms slung round each other, and Con and Darryl were packing up to go.

"Can we leave our tents and stuff here?" I said. "Then we won't be weighed down with clobber."

"Hope Karen and Cliff manage to take their eyes off each other long enough to make sure nobody nicks nothing," said Michael.

So when we set off we felt as free as birds. It was a beautiful day. But as we flew along the cycle track with the breeze blowing and the sun shining, I couldn't have had any idea what a beautiful day it was going to be, in a way that had nothing to do with the weather at all.

18 · Tent-Talk

Snug in our little tent that night, Con and me whispered.

"What sort of day did you have?"

"Fabulous," she said. It was the first time I'd ever heard her say that. She wasn't much for straight enjoyment, Con wasn't – if she did enjoy herself, she didn't like admitting it somehow, she'd always shut it off and say "Not bad" or "It was okay in its way," or something. Now she lay on her back looking up at the roof of the tent and said, "– Just fabulous," again.

"What was it like – the island?"

"Heaven."

"And the birds? Were they nice?"

"There was one hot-house," she said, all kind of dreamy, not a bit like her usual self, "with all sorts of tropical stuff in it, huge leaves and great big juicy-looking flowers, all reds and purples, looking like they wanted to eat you up. I mean, honest – they had their tongues sticking out to catch you. And the heat just closed round you, all steamy. I felt like Tarzan's mate or something. I wanted to pick up a vine and start swinging through the trees."

"That's just like at Kew then," I said. They took us to the hot-house at Kew from school once. Too hot for me by half.

"But there's no birds at Kew," she said. "In this one they were everywhere, lovely bright-coloured ones, some big and some so small I thought they were big insects at first. Sucking out of the flowers with their little wings beating so fast you couldn't see 'em, even. . . . And others flashing about round your head. We stopped in there for an hour. We pretended we was in Africa, in the jungle. The smells were something else, too. *Exotic*."

"Wasn't it all hot and sticky?"

"Sticky? It was great, I told you! I'm never hot enough usually. That's my trouble. Feel my hand now."

I took her hand. It was cold as ice, like a dead fish.

"Yuk!"

"You see? I'm cold-blooded. I think I'll leave England and go south. I told Darryl. He said he felt the same. It's just too cold in these northern countries, you spend half your energy trying to keep warm." I was kind of aut">mically rubbing her hand, like Mum does mine if I come in cold without my gloves. But Con took it off me. "It's no use," she said. "I rub 'em sometimes myself, but they only get cold again. Darryl's got very warm hands, have you noticed?"

"No I haven't! How come you found that out?"

"He held my hand a lot while we was walking around," she said. "It started in the cold part, where the penguins and that are – they got ice-caves; not real ice of course, it's only got up like ice, but they keep the temperature cold for the Arctic birds, and I was shivering while we walked through there and Darryl took my hand and kind of stuffed it into his pocket. His hand's naturally warm."

"Not surprising."

"What you mean?" she asked quickly.

"He's a warm sort of person," I said. "Shy, but he's got a warm nature, I've noticed."

She didn't say anything for a bit. Then she said, "One thing about him, he's very gentle. I mean you can't imagine him – you know, hitting anybody." I didn't say anything. I knew what she was thinking about. After a while she turned towards me in the dark and said, "What about you, where did you go?"

I'd been waiting for her to ask.

"Best day I ever had," I said.

That was going it a bit, I admit – I've had a good few nice times in my life. There'd been holidays at Frinton and even one in Wales, when the shop'd had a good year, and there were always good Christmases (when there weren't too many rows). Mum was good at Christmas. We always did things traditional, starting with Midnight Mass at Our Lady of Lourdes, and hot drinks with a drop of something in them so we always had a good sleep. Then waking up to stockings.

Every year Mum says, "Now you big ones are far too old for all that nonsense. It'll be just Tracy and Lily this year" – or, lately, "just Lily". And we'd all set up a terrible howl and clown around pretending to be little kids – Sean put on a nappy last year and lay on the floor sucking his thumb and howling till

Mum gave in! Then there'd be late lunch and afterwards we'd go for a walk – Dad always insisted, and we always went to the same place, Acton Park, and the boys played football.

It was the only time Vlady ever would, and he was a lousy player of course. He could scarcely kick the ball. Sometimes if Sean sent it at him hard he'd pretend to be scared of it and jump over it or dodge out of the way, hands over his head. Sean would send him up rotten and we'd all stand there yelling with laughter while Vlady put on a big act of being ashamed and ran off to get the ball back. Sometimes we'd all play, us girls too, all breaking the rules on purpose, picking the ball up and playing pig-in-the-middle with it while old Sean did his nut.

Then we'd go home for tea and Mum's Christmas cake, all black and gluggy inside from all the whisky she'd poured in the little black holes in the bottom of it for weeks before, enough to make you drunk, and with the same little figures of Father Christmas and his reindeer, and a tree, that's been on our cakes for years and years. Then we'd go to the evening service and. . . .

Bloody hell. How did I get onto all that lot? I was talking about my good day in that village. . . . Bloody hell. I'm crying now. You'd think, just because of what I've done, there was never going to be Christmas any more.

To get on with it then. So Connie of course asked, "What was so special?" and I told her about Gouda and then how we'd gone on to a little place a few miles away where they used to have a lot of witches, or what they thought were witches. This village found it was getting a bad name through burning more poor old girls there than anywhere else in Holland. It was hurting trade. So they had this idea. They made a law that everyone who was accused of witchcraft had to be brought to their public weighing house to be weighed. The person had to be dressed in a witch's costume made of paper, and have a paper broom. Then they'd weigh her, and announce she was too heavy to ride on a broom stick! They'd give the poor old cow a certificate to say she was too fat to be a witch and off she'd go.

Con wanted to know if the scales and that, that they'd weighed them with, were still there, and I said not only that, but you could have yourself weighed and get a certificate to say you weren't a witch! I'd even got one myself! I switched on my torch and showed it to her.

"Cor," she said, half-joking.

"And then," I went on, warming up now, "we had a meal at a little café, not the Tourist menu, and Michael treated me, and we talked."

"What about?"

"Him mostly. He's going to stick with his building job, and try and study architecture at night school or even on Open University. He's got one A-level already. In history. Like me."

"What you mean, like you?"

"I mean it's my best subject, too. I could've got an O-level in it if I'd tried. And in English too, I bet."

"So what stopped you, eh?"

"I dunno," I said. "That's what he asked too. Why I don't stop on at school. To be honest I never even gave it a thought. I mean, all our lot's leaving, aren't they."

"I might not."

"Get away! You staying on?" I couldn't believe it.

"I said I might."

"But you just said you were leaving England!"

"I didn't say *now*. I said some time." She paused a bit and then said, "Of course I can't stay on, though. I'll have to leave home and take a job. I can't stick it at home much longer, certainly not another two years."

"Well I could," I said. And Dad'd be pleased. . . . Funny, I never considered it. . . . Going back to school next September, though. Could I stand it? We lay in the dark. I was trying to think ahead, but I couldn't; my head was too full of today.

"Listen though, let me tell you the rest. So we talked, and we found out we got a lot in common, him and me— "

"You mean, apart from both having A-levels in history?"

"Shurrup you. Of course I haven't half his brain— "

"Oh Jesus, Trace!"

"What?"

"Don't be so bloody humble! Your brain's all right, nothing wrong with your brain except you never give it enough to do."

"How'd you work that out?"

"Well. I've seen you, haven't I, sitting in class for four years, or rather, laying about in class in your case, doing the least you could get away with— "

"I never! I did my best—"

"Oh yeah? What about in English? Just because old Nelson told you off once for your spelling, you lay down and played dead. Never did another stroke in her lessons. Did you? A whole year wasted for one bad mark. You're just stupid, you are."

"That's what I said. I got no head."

"That's one excuse for just being bone bloody idle."

If I'd been less happy and more in the mood to tangle, I'd've given her what-for, but as it was I just shut up for a bit. And in the silence it came clear that what she was telling me off for was being brighter than I thought I was. So after a bit I said, "You think I'm not so thick, really?"

"I never thought you were thick. Did he try anything?"

"Eh?"

"Michael."

"No! He doesn't fancy *me*."

"If you think that, maybe you are thick after all."

I rolled right over on my side to face her.

"Connie, what are you getting at? Michael – fancy me?"

"You really didn't notice? Why d'you think he hates Kev so much?"

"Because he's a bit of a tearaway, writes on walls and that."

"That too. . . . Do you know Michael had us all round that bleeding statue in the dead of night, scraping and scrubbing away. . . ." I started laughing, I couldn't help it.

"D'you get it off?"

"I dunno, do I, we could hardly see what we was doing in the pitch dark. . . ." We muffled our giggles in our bundles of clothes. When we calmed down a bit, she said, "Darryl did."

"What, started necking? And you let him?"

"It was in that hot-house. I felt all funny. I had to kiss someone, and he was there."

"Was it nice?"

"Nice! Listen, Trace, you'll never get your English O-level till you stop saying 'nice' all the time. It's a nothing word. Of course it wasn't 'nice'. What does it mean, 'nice'? It was. . . . " She

153

stopped. Then she rolled away from me, sudden. "I dunno how it was," she mumbled.

"Did it turn you on?" I persisted.

"Well, if it did," she said, "it wasn't because of Darryl. Take more than some spotty sixteen-year-old to turn me on. It was those bloody birds and the heat and the scent of those jungle flowers. I'd've been turned on necking with King Kong in there if you want to know."

I felt she didn't want to talk any more so I shut up. I didn't either, to say the true, I just wanted to lie quiet and think about my day. Riding through the villages with Michael, and stopping to look at things, and being weighed on the witches' scales, and later, going to another place, near a river, where we saw some silver jewellery being made. Filigree it's called, very fine silver wire twisted into shapes like tiny bits of lace.

I reached out my hand and groped about in my pile of clothes. Pinned to my T-shirt I found it, a little hard shape – a butterfly brooch, smaller than a real butterfly. Delicate. Perfect. He'd bought it for me and pinned it on. If Kev'd done something like that (not that he ever had), he'd have tried to touch me up when he was pinning it on, but not Michael. He did his best *not* to touch me, but his fingers just couldn't help themselves. I could feel them now, as light as if a real butterfly had landed on me for a second. . . .

I thought of Kev groping me in that doorway after the disco, and then I thought, if Michael ever put his hand right on me like that, on purpose, to show he fancied me – but I couldn't think about it. It couldn't ever happen. I mean he'd never do it, and if he did I couldn't have stood it. I felt hot and weak just thinking about it. Much more than I did when Kev actually did it. And that was bad enough, though somehow I found I didn't like thinking about that either, now.

19 · Turned Right Off

Michael woke me in the morning. He did it by reaching into our tent and taking hold of my foot. I wasn't in my sleeping-bag because it was too hot, and my pyjama leg was rucked right up. First thing I knew, I felt this hand touching my foot and giving it a little shake. Or maybe more of a little stroke. It gave me something like an electric shock. I jerked up and hit my head on the roof-pole. Everything sparkled round Michael's face in the tent opening.

"Time to get up," he said. He was smiling at me.

Then he went. I woke Connie. We got dressed half-lying down. I still felt a bit dizzy, though, and when I crawled out and stood up I nearly fell down again.

There was a lot of bustling about, packing, while Karen got breakfast. Getting dead good with the old frying pan, Karen was – way beyond hard-boiled eggs now, it was sausages and bacon and fried bread – you name it. Michael and me had filled up our side-bags with groceries on the way home last night, and while we sat around eating in the sun we had a grand settling-up. I'd paid my own way except for the first couple of nights when Michael had been organising and paying for everything, so I just said to him, "What do I owe you for the first night in the camping site?"

"That's okay."

"What do you mean, okay? I got to cough up my share!"

In the end he gave in, and I fished out my purse and paid my debts. As I put the money into his hand I got that funny shock again, and he got it too seemingly, because he jerked his hand and didn't look me in the eye. I thought, *God, what's happening here?* I might not have even noticed it if it hadn't been for what Con'd said the night before about Michael fancying me. Could it be? I kept giving him little looks out the sides of my eyes, taking him in as if I'd never seen him before.

He looked different from before somehow. I remembered

155

something Mary said once when I was asking her whatever she saw in some boy or other she was going out with. Face like the flatside of a gumboot. She said, "You don't see 'em the same way when you're in love." I made throw-up noises I remember, thinking she was too soppy to be true, but now I looked at Michael and I felt a bit soppy myself. All brown – the rest of his face had kind of caught up with his freckles – and his hair a bit longer than before, down his neck, curling.

But the thing that got me most was his body. Must be humping stuff on the building site that gave him those big shoulders. He had lovely round arms too. Specially at the top, the skin over his muscles so smooth and silky I wanted to stroke it. . . . I looked down at my own arm. That looked brown and silky too. I wondered if he wanted to stroke that. I remembered how he'd touched my foot that morning, while I was still asleep, how I'd felt it in my morning dream. . . .

"Come on, you lot, time to be moving."

I didn't want to move. I wanted to lie there dreaming. But there was no time. We all had to help rolling the tents up.

While we were busy at it, I noticed something funny. There was Karen rolling up one tent, and Cliff rolling up another. Back to back. I went over to help Karen and we had our heads together, kneeling on the sand, and I muttered in her ear, "What's up with you two?"

She shook her head as if a fly was biting her. "Nothing, what you mean?" Dead snarky with it.

"Why aren't you rolling with Cliff?"

"Rolling with *Cliff*? *Rolling* with him? I've done rolling with that creep, I can tell you that for a start!" she said, loud enough for him to hear.

"What's he done now?"

"None of your business!" she snapped. "And I can do this on my own, thanks very much," and she turned her back on me too.

Talk about on again, off again! And at the same time, there's old stuck-up Con, rolling away with Darryl, cosy as you like, even giggling together a bit. Wonderful what a hot-house and a few birds'll do. Not that I'd have bet on it to last.

"Well," said Darryl, "last time for this time." He stood up and dusted the sand off himself, looking round at us all. "I don't

156

know about you lot, but I'm going to do this again soon as I've saved some cash."

"Soon as you've earned it, you mean," I said.

"Oh I'll earn it all right! Don't worry about that. France for me next time round." And he looked sideways at Con.

"Smashing food in France," she said.

H'm!

At eight o'clock we set off, whizzing down the track beside the traffic. *Goodbye Holland!* I was thinking. Just imagine, by tonight we'd be home, I'd be telling the family all about everything. I felt older. I'd found out more in that week than in a solid year at that stupid school. Must be what they mean about foreign travel broadening the mind. And my body was better too – not broader (I hoped!) but healthier. I was a gorgeous colour (Mary wouldn't half be jealous!) and I didn't get leg-ache at all now.

I was in a good mood, all excited about the boat-trip and getting home, as we turned into the docks at the Hook. Our boat was waiting for us. And suddenly I saw that so was someone else.

Kev.

This is going to sound dead stupid, but I'd forgotten all about him. Well, almost. I mean, he'd dropped right into the back of my mind. The front part being full of Michael. When I saw him standing there – Kev I mean – outside the customs shed with his bike, waiting for us, my heart did a flop. Not a flip – a flop, a kind of flabby flop.

Of course nobody else felt like that, except maybe Michael who was still narked about him leaving me the way he did. The other two boys let out a cheer and zoomed up to him, yelling and teasing. "There's a lad, then! Where'd you get to, eh? What you been getting up to?" and all that, like he was some kind of folk-hero. Karen was acting all feminine, I noticed – flirting with him to get back at Cliff, I suppose. Even Con gave him a welcome in her way. But he was looking over them all, at me.

"'Lo, Trace," he said, a bit sheepish.

"'Lo."

I didn't want to say too much to him, so I just wheeled my bike into the customs. He came after me, but I kept turned away, and

Michael stuck with me so Kev couldn't talk to me alone. Of course I knew I wouldn't be able to keep that up, and sure enough, when we got on the boat and everybody scattered, I found myself up on the highest deck with him climbing up the ladder after me. I leaned on the rail looking at the horizon.

"Are you not speaking to me or something?" he had the cheek to ask.

"What if I'm not? D'you blame me?"

"What did I do that was so terrible you had to run off without a bloody dickybird?"

I turned to him then all right. Turned *on* him rather.

"Don't you know what you did? You call that—" I nearly said "nice" but I remembered what Con said and changed it to— "decent, to piss off like that when I was sleeping and leave me all on my tod half the night in a strange flat?"

He hung his head. "I thought you'd sleep through till morning," he said. "You wouldn't have liked it anyway."

"I believe that!" I snapped back. "Disgusting, I'll bet! But you'd rather see that cheap dirty rubbish than be with me, wouldn't you, you and your new pals? You know what they were, don't you – them two? Porn merchants, that's what. No, not just merchants, they actually *give* the merchants what to merch!"

"What you on about, merch? What's 'merch'?"

"Flog, then. Those two take photos of girls with their backsides hanging out of key-holes, on motorbikes—"

I was getting all mixed up and he was starting to laugh at me. But I wasn't about to back down.

"—And talking of flogging," I said, "did they show you their collection? Mucky sods, that's what they are! I can just imagine what kind of dirty old men buy the pictures they take – a bunch of rotten sadists!"

He looked dead sullen now. "I dunno what you're talking about. They was okay – good blokes. Lot older than us, they didn't have to take us on, give us a place to kip for free, not to mention—" He stopped, but I'd caught on, or thought I had.

"Don't tell me they treated you to the clubs and that as well?"

"So what?"

"So where's your pride? I wouldn't've taken nothing from

them, not if I'd known what sort they were! What were they up to, anyhow?"

"They wasn't up to nothing! They was just being friendly."

"Oh yeah? Must've been something behind it. That sort don't give nothing away." I noticed he'd gone red. "Oh, so that was it, was it?"

"What?" he said quickly, looking up at me with his eyes kind of startled (I'm only remembering the details now, looking back. I didn't take them in at the time, I was too angry).

"They were on at you to get me to pose for 'em! Wasn't that it?"

He seemed to relax, and laughed a bit. "Get away," he said. "As if I would."

"Wouldn't put it past you," I mumbled, although I really believed him. He wasn't that bad, Kev, though I knew now he'd do a good lot if there was money in it.

"Look, Trace," he said, all gentle, trying to get round me. "Let's forget it. I admit I shouldn't've left you. I felt bad all the time; I wanted to come back but it was awkward, I mean with me being their guest and that. And I meant to make it up to you next day, but then you'd gone, hadn't you. I wish you'd've left me a note, I was dead worried about you."

"I bet!"

"I was. Course I was." And he tried to grab me, but I jerked away. "Can't we make it up?" he said, blowing down my neck the way I used to go for.

But I was noticing something. Before, when he'd come this close, I'd been all in a state, but now I wasn't. Not a bit. I just wanted to get away from him. He turned me right off suddenly. I even rubbed my ear where I'd felt his breath, and when he tried again to put his arm round me I just ran away from him, and practically slid down the ladder like a fireman I was in such a hurry to get back to the others. It wasn't even that I wouldn't forgive him – I'd almost forgot all about Amsterdam and that. I just didn't want to be alone with him any more.

He came after me, and caught me by the arm half-way along the deck.

"Tracy, I forgot! I've got something for you!"

I stopped. He'd never given me anything – ever. I wanted to

see what he thought would make it up to me for the way he'd acted.

He had his rucksack on the deck and was groping in it. "Bet you'll be pleased to see this!" he said, all bright-eyed and full of nice surprises.

And handed me my pump.

20 · Dogs and Coppers

We all stood in a line, against the back railing of the boat, watching Holland sort of sinking into the sea behind us. None of us said anything, but we were all a bit sad. We wouldn't forget that holiday in a hurry.

One thing I did wonder, standing there in the salt spray. Why Holland in the first place? I mean, how did we decide to go there and not, say, to France? I racked my brains trying to remember who first mentioned Holland of all places. Well, it had to be Kev, didn't it? I mean the whole thing was his idea.

He was standing next to me, but a little way along the rail, staring down into all that churned-up white sea coming out from under the back of the boat. He looked put-down and miserable, and although I was still furious I thought it was silly to go on not speaking.

"Hey, Kev," I said, above the noise of the engines and the water. He looked up at me. His face was all hard, but then it always went like that if he felt he'd been got at. "What made you think of going to Holland to begin with?"

"I was just wondering that," said Karen. And she went around the back of Cliff and stood, all come-and-get-me-I'm-free between me and Kev, looking up at him.

Kev shrugged. "I dunno. Just wanted to see it, that's all."

"But why not France, say, or Spain? All that hot sun and sexy women?" Karen said, googling her eyes at him. He gave her a cool look.

"Maybe I'd rather have a pair of clogs and a windmill," he said, and turned back to the sea as if she wasn't there.

We spent hours on the boat playing cards and pencil and paper games, all but Kev and Cliff who played with the one-arm bandits. That took care of any odd coins they had left over. Michael seemed to be sticking fairly close to me. Once, he went off to queue up for some tea. Asked me if I wanted a cup. I knew by now what it costs on those boats so I said no thanks. But he

161

brought me one anyway, and a fresh roll and butter and jam. So
then Darryl took the hint and went and got the same for Con.
Poor old Karen! Women's lib time for her – never happened to
her in her life before, I bet. I offered her half mine but she turned
up her nose at it and left our game to "go and get some air" – she
said. I guessed she'd gone looking for Kev so she could flirt with
him in front of Cliff.

At last Michael looked at his watch and said we might be able
to see England if we went up on deck. It had gone all gloomy
outside, as if we'd left the sun behind in Holland. The sky was
low and grey and it was raining a sort of misty rain. We put on
our cagoules though, and went out on the front deck. Couldn't
see much ahead of course – there was even a bit of fog on the
water.

"What price biking in this?" said Darryl.

The ship's syren hooted. Saddest sound there is. I felt my heart
sinking somehow. It was as if I knew I was going into some kind
of misery. I shivered, and Michael suddenly put his arm round
me. Lovely strong warm arm. I felt better in one second flat.

*

We docked at Harwich in mid-afternoon. Lugged all our stuff
and our bikes off, and headed for the customs sheds. As we were
walking along the quayside, Michael suddenly said, "Look over
there!"

We looked. Waiting at the far end, where the cars would come
off, were some policemen with dogs on leads.

"Who do you think they're after?" Cliff asked.

"Smugglers," said Con.

"What they want the dogs for, to chase 'em if they make a run
for it?"

"Don't you know?" asked Michael. "Those Alsatians are
specially trained. I bet the fuzz have had a tip-off."

"What sort of tip-off?" said Kev.

"Must be expecting someone to try and get drugs in."

"Drugs?"

"Yeah – the hard stuff. The dogs can sniff it out."

"Great!" said Cliff. "Good for a laugh, specially if they catch
someone. Why don't we slide along there and watch?"

"Yeah, let's!" we said.

162

"Well, I'm not bothering to come—" Kev shouted after us. But we were half-running now, hoping to see some fun, and we hardly noticed he wasn't with us.

When we reached the other end, we came up against a barrier, but we could see everything. We just stood there, holding our loaded bikes, watching while the cars came slowly out of a big opening in the back of the boat, bumping onto the dockside and queueing up at the customs.

Two of the coppers led their dogs forward and they stood near the cars. Another one was still standing near us, on the other side of the barrier. We were chatting away and seemingly we got on his nerves, because he turned to us and said, "What are you lot hanging about for? You'd better take yourselves off, it's not a circus laid on for your benefit."

Of course he only took that tone because some of us still looked a bit punkish. It made me mad, because we weren't doing any harm, and I felt like giving him a piece of my mind. But Michael got there first with a bit of the other cheek.

"Are we in your way, Officer?" he asked, sweetly.

"I didn't say that, did I?"

"We've read about the way your dogs work. Marvellous. I'm a dog-fancier myself. I'd appreciate it if you'd let us watch how they do it."

While he was saying this, he'd reached over the barrier to stroke the third dog's head. I wouldn't have dared – savage-looking thing – but they say dogs know who to trust. It stuck its tongue out and sort of panted up at Michael, all loving.

The policeman looked a bit annoyed.

"Don't handle her, she don't like strangers," he said, although it was clear as daylight she liked this one.

"Sorry," said Michael at once, and took his hand away. The dog shifted on its rear-end so it could poke its nose through a hole in the wire, looking for Michael's hand.

Suddenly it went all stiff. You could see its tail had stopped wagging. And the same second the policeman changed too. I can't explain it, he just went tense, his head shifted in a little jerk towards us and his eyes got beady. The dog's bottom came slowly away from the ground. It stood up on stiff legs, its nose still through the wire as if it was stuck there, and you could hear it

163

going *sniff-sniff-sniff*. Very sharply it pulled its nose out, moved along the barrier, and stuck it back in further down. Right opposite where I was.

The copper stretched his arm so the lead wouldn't pull. He didn't have to move. The dog sniffed like mad. Then it pulled its nose out, threw up its head and started to bark.

I jumped back. It gave me such a fright! It was barking straight at me! And one second later, that copper had vaulted right over the barrier. The dog jumped after him. It made a rush at my bike. Next minute there it was, pointing its black nose straight at my pump. And the copper had hold of me as if he wanted to pinch my arm in half.

The nightmare had begun.

21 · My Ordeal

I've got to skip here. Not that I don't like remembering what happened next – I can't. It was all so mixed up and horrible. I don't even remember seeing them opening up the pump and finding those long, thin packets inside. I saw them later, but not when they first found them.

I wasn't crying or anything, I just – well, it was like a blackout. A blank. There was a lot of noise going on – barking and shouting (I do remember Michael shouting, perhaps because he hardly ever did and now he seemed to go crazy) and Con's voice in my ear saying something like "Take it easy, take it easy." But really I can't remember details until I found myself in a little room with a woman in uniform – not a police uniform – standing facing me telling me to get undressed.

I couldn't at first. It wasn't that I wouldn't – I could hardly move myself. I felt so strange. I just stared at her like an idiot.

"Come along, I'll help you," she said, and stepped towards me.

"No!" I shouted, waking up suddenly and with the same awful dizzy feeling you get. "Don't you touch me!"

"Then do it by yourself. Everything off."

I do remember this part, all too clearly, but I won't describe it. It was just – horrible. She didn't only make me strip right off. She wanted to examine me. Like a doctor. I couldn't believe it. When I saw what she was at, I backed away against the wall and started screaming. Outside I could hear Michael's voice shouting, "What's going on, what are they doing to her?" and then right near the door, calling, "Tracy! Tracy!"

I felt wild, like an animal. I stopped yelling, and started kicking out at this woman with her horrible transparent glove.

"Don't be so silly, it won't hurt," she said.

Hurt! That's all they think you mind about, is pain. I thought I was going mad. I didn't know yet what had happened, I just thought the whole world had turned against me. Any normal pain would have been better than that.

In the end she had to get someone in to help her because I fought tooth and nail. But they did it finally, what they had to do. Then they turned round and tried to be nice, and calm me down, but it was no good, I was all to pieces by then and so was Michael outside, by the sound of it. Later on I felt ashamed of carrying on like that and getting him so upset, imagining heaven knows what from the way I was yelling (though it couldn't have been much worse than the truth). But at the time I couldn't control myself and that was that.

They had to get a doctor to me and he gave me an injection. That stopped me crying. Someone helped me get dressed again. Finally they led me out of that hateful little room. Michael was waiting. He jumped up and rushed at me the minute he saw me.

We looked at each other. I can't describe that look. His eyes were shocked, a bit like my father's eyes. He didn't touch me, not with his hands. But his look was like – well, this sounds silly, but it made me feel like the night I came home all frozen from the Music Mill and climbed into bed and found the hot blanket on. Only more. I think even if I hadn't had that injection, that look Michael gave me would have calmed me down. He didn't speak – I don't think he could, any more than I could – but his eyes said two words: "I'm here."

They took us outside into the street and there was a car waiting. A police car. We got in the back. A policeman and a woman was in front. Our stuff was put in the boot, except our bikes. I couldn't have cared less. I felt so tired I nearly dropped off the minute I sat down. Michael didn't talk, but he put his arm round me and held my hand. I leant against him. I had no thoughts in my head.

They drove us through the streets, I suppose, though my eyes were closed and I think I dozed off. Next thing, Michael was helping me out. There was a police station. Up the steps, into a sort of waiting-room. Questions. Now I remember there were a lot of them before, while I was in that funny blank state – and even now I couldn't say much, just my name and that I didn't know anything about any drug or how it could have got in my pump. But even through whatever that doctor gave me, through the shock, something was starting to move in my head, beginning to click. I'd have to start thinking soon. I didn't want to, but I'd have to. I knew it.

The first part I couldn't put off thinking about was Dad and Mum. Because the police were going to phone them. They'd even got the name and phone number out of me before I'd gathered my wits. It seemed they couldn't charge me, or whatever it is they do, until my dad was with me, on account of me being under age. So far, Michael'd stood in for him, but for the formal bit he wouldn't do.

At the thought of what Mum'd feel like when that phone call came (Dad wouldn't even be at home, it was still shop-hours) some of the fog cleared. I grabbed Michael, who was sitting beside me.

"Michael, don't let them phone! You go. You tell them."

He looked at me. His poor face! I saw what he was thinking. He *undertook* us, we were his responsibility. Now I was asking him to knock on our door and face Dad and tell him I'd been arrested, that he'd got to come and bail me or I couldn't come home.

I thought of course he'd say no, that he'd say he wanted to stay with me. And I wanted him to – how I wanted him to! The thought of being left there by myself was so awful I could hardly stand it. But after a minute or two of looking at me, he gave my arm a squeeze and stood up without a word. He turned away and started to walk towards the door. I felt myself wanting to scream out to him, "Come back! Don't leave me!" I didn't, but as if I had, as if he'd heard my thought, he stopped and came back and bent over me, holding my shoulder.

"Be brave," he whispered to me, so soft I hardly heard. Then he kissed me, the side of my head. Then he walked away again. This time I didn't want to call him back. I felt strong inside, for the moment anyway. He was so strong he made me strong.

*

They were quite good to me in that place. They took me into a room with ordinary furniture in it, a settee-thing and a couple of hard chairs. The woman let me sit on the settee. I was shivering again so she brought me a blanket to wrap round me, and a cup of tea, and a sandwich. I drank the tea. It was in one of those squudgy throw-away cups. I kept biting pieces out of it, my teeth were chattering so much. I spilt a lot of tea so they brought me another cup. I couldn't eat the sandwich.

There was a policewoman with me now. She came and sat beside me and put her arm round me.

"Tracy, would you like to talk to me?"

"What about?"

"They found drugs on you. Do you really not know how they got there?"

Crafty cow! I pulled myself away from her. I curled up in a corner of the settee with my back to her. I couldn't think straight, and I knew better than to say anything while I was in that state.

The woman went and sat in her chair again. When I took a peep at her, she wasn't even looking at me, she was reading.

I uncurled a bit. There were things I wanted to know, too.

"Where's my friends?"

She looked up again. "They've gone back to London."

I suppose she saw my face, because she added quickly, "They had to, Tracy. They didn't want to leave you – especially the little dark one, Connie is it? She wanted to stay with you, but it's not allowed. When you've finished here, you'll go to London too, with your dad. And then you'll be able to see your friends again."

"Am I arrested?"

"Well, yes, sort of. I mean, yes. But there's no need to be frightened. Nobody's going to hurt you."

I wasn't bothered about that. All I could think of was what Dad was going to feel like. Hurt? Not the word for it. And Mum. And Vlady. . . . When I got down to what Lily would feel like I felt myself starting to thaw out inside, and the tears pushing behind my eyes.

But just before I started blubbing, feeling so sorry for everyone, I thought of someone I didn't have to feel sorry for. And the tears stopped.

That rotten, lousy, shitty, stinking Kev! What a bastard. What a *rat*! Of course! It was clear as daylight now I'd got round to thinking about it. *He*'d pinched my pump, that night they all went to the nightclub. Those two creeps had told him to. They'd hollowed it out and put the stuff in and he'd brought it back, all innocent, and lumbered me with it to bring in for him. Once I'd been through customs with it, he'd've made some excuse to get it off me, or he'd have pinched it again, and passed the drugs on to whoever it was in London. And got God knows how much money for it.

Money. . . . Here, hang about. He hadn't been too badly off even before. I'd had my suspicions about how he'd earned that lot, too. What if it had all been a put-up job, right from the beginning? From the London end? What if – now I was using my head and wasn't everything clicking into place! – what if *that* was why he'd wanted to go to Holland from the off?

"Do you catch a lot of people coming from Holland with drugs?" I asked this woman.

"Goodness me, yes! At least once a week. Amsterdam's a very big centre. Our Chief Inspector recently caught two men bringing in enough heroin to fill a whole suitcase – about five million pounds' worth. They'll probably be sent away for fifteen or twenty years." She seemed proud of that. Then she looked at me and her face got softer. "Oh, but don't you worry. Yours is very small beer by comparison. I expect you just brought cannabis, didn't you? Not hard stuff?"

At it again – trying to get me to confess. I said, for about the tenth time, "I don't know anything about it. I never even saw it."

"I have. Packed down your pump in long thin tubes. Quite ingenious really. Was it you who thought of that?"

No. It wasn't me. It was my lousy boyfriend, that's who it was. It was him let me in for this. That horrible search they did on me, and all. I'll pay you out, Kevin Blake; don't you think I'll shield you, don't sit there on that train thinking "She won't peach on me" because she bloody will, first chance she gets!

Well, here was a chance, wasn't it? Why didn't I turn nark and tell this woman, with her hungry eyes, all about it? I opened my mouth, and closed it again. No. Better wait for Dad to get here.

After a while I fell asleep, sitting up. I felt the woman kind of spreading me out on the settee, putting my feet up. She was quite gentle, putting the blanket over me and tucking me in. I wondered if Mum would do that tonight. Then I dropped down and down into blackness.

22 · Dad

Dad came. It took him about five hundred years, but he did come at last.

I'd only slept for about half the five hundred years. The rest of the time I was awake. Waiting. Thinking. I swear I never did so much thinking (or feeling) in all my life till then.

They brought me dinner on a tray, and it didn't look bad, but when I tried to eat some I nearly choked. Honest, my throat closed up, I'd have been sick if I'd forced myself. More tea went down though, and I didn't bite the cup this time (maybe because they brought me a proper china one). The policewoman didn't ask any more questions. She did try to chat me up a bit, asking about school and our trip and that, but I didn't trust her so I just grunted answers. I'd have liked to be nicer, but I couldn't. I wasn't even there, really. I was on the London-to-Harwich train with Dad.

Remember how I said I could never practise things beforehand, like Karen? How I just let them happen? Not this time. This was too horrible just to let it come on me without getting ready as much as I could. I tried every way of telling him. I imagined him taking it every way I thought he might – being angry, being sad, being kind. Being quiet. That was the one I dreaded worst, but they were all bad. Sometimes as the hours (years I mean) went by, I imagined the scenes so clearly, I cried.

At last the door opened, and there he was.

A policeman let him in, and signalled the policewoman. She got up without a word and went out and they shut the door.

Dad didn't notice anything but me. He came straight across the room and took me in his arms and held me there, tight to his little round stomach, the safest place I knew in the world – safer than rolled up in bed, safer than Michael's arms even. If I could have just stopped there forever, with my face hidden on his shoulder! But it couldn't last long. He held me away and looked in my face and then we sat down on the settee together.

"Tell me," he said. "Tell me everything. In detail. Leave nothing out."

I told him everything. Well. Not everything. Not the whips. I couldn't, somehow. And not me getting drunk on Tracy's Multicoloured Gobstop. But I told about Neils and Yohan and that they took dirty pictures and that Kev went out with them and left me, and that Michael'd done all he could for me, including warn me not to go with Kev alone, not to leave the group.

"Also I warn you that."

"Yeah, Dad. I know."

"Why you always go your own way, Tracy." It wasn't a question, so I didn't answer it. So far it wasn't going like any of the ways I'd prepared. Does it ever?

"You have told the police all this?" he asked next.

"No."

"Why not?"

"I wanted to tell you first."

"What you mean, perhaps, you don't want to shop your friend."

It always sounds so funny when Dad uses slang, but this time I didn't laugh. "I hate him," I said. "I want to shop him!"

"So why you didn't?"

"I told you! I wanted to talk to you first."

He gazed at me with his sad pale-blue eyes.

"You still like him very much?"

"Dad! Are you listening to me? I hate him, he's horrible! You don't know what I been through because of him!" Remembering it myself, I began to cry, but he stopped me by not being sympathetic.

"There's no use to that," he said. "I'm sorry for your bad time, my girl, but it is no point to cry. Now we go through the formality, and then I take you home. On the train we talk. We talk about Kevin."

"I don't want to talk about him!"

"I want to talk about him," he said, very firm.

They booked me, or bailed me, or whatever they do. I let Dad do everything. They said they'd got to have the stuff in the pump tested and then I'd have to appear in court in Harwich. It might not be very soon, they said, a matter of weeks.

171

"Weeks!" I said. Think of waiting weeks with that hanging over you!

"The wheels of the law grind small, but they grind exceeding slow," said the policeman, as if it was some kind of a joke.

Dad said, all of a sudden, "I want to see it."

The man sat back. "No, I'm afraid—"

Dad leaned over the desk. His fist was closed, trembling. "She brought it in this country. My daughter. I want to see what it looks like."

The policeman looked from Dad to me. Then he stood up. "I'll see what I can do," he said. "It's a bit irregular."

While he was out of the room, Dad turned to me. He whispered, "Perhaps I can tell what is it. If it is cannabis, that is nothing so bad. But if it is heroin, we must get a good lawyer."

I remembered what the woman had said about the men with the suitcase, the five million pounds, the long sentences. "No, Dad!" I said. "It's not heroin! It can't be. It's just pot, she said that's all it was!"

"Who said that?"

"The woman! She said it was probably only pot!"

"Probably? Then she doesn't know."

The policeman came back with a box. He took the lid off and let us look inside. There were the long narrow packets. One had come open a bit at one end and a little white powder had spilt out. Dad stared at it. Then he looked up at the man. "What will happen to this?"

He rolled his lips inside his teeth. "We send it to the forensic lab. They'll tell us for sure if it's what we think it is."

My heart dropped into my stomach. It was heroin. Dad didn't say anything. He took my arm and led me out of the place. There was a police car to take us to the station. My bike was there waiting. The driver of the car helped Dad to put my rucksack and bike on the train. It all passed in a sort of mist. I was all – it's hard to explain – I was living up in my head again, with thoughts, with pictures. Me in the court. Being sentenced to twenty years. Mum crying. Me in prison – *Within These Walls*, and no Googie Withers there to look after me, either. Shut up with delinquents. Thieves and prostitutes. Murderers. . . .

But no. They wouldn't. Because I'd shop Kev, and then they'd know. They'd send him down instead of me. Men's prisons are worse of course, because men are worse, and more of them go inside so the jails are more crowded and far worse things happen there. I saw a programme once about American prisons; there was this big black criminal, telling young boys what was in store for them if they got sent in there. Terrible things. Dad switched off after a bit, saying, "That's not for you to see. America is another world anyway, everything is better and worse than here. . . ." Still, Borstals were no holiday, and there was this new idea I'd heard about, something about giving young offenders a short sharp shock. Of course, that's just what Kev needed, and maybe not so short, either. . . .

We were sitting in the train and it was going. I hadn't even noticed it pull out of Harwich, but now we were rattling along. It was nearly night. The countryside was flat like Holland, but not like it any other way. This was England and even in the dusk it couldn't be anywhere else. I was home and Dad was sitting opposite me and I was in dead, dead trouble.

"Now," he said. "Kevin."

"Why do we have to talk about him?"

"He is at the base of it all, that's why."

After a long pause I heard myself say, "I can't know that."

"What other?"

"Perhaps," I said slowly, "perhaps he didn't know anything about it. Perhaps Neils and Yohan just made use of him."

Dad was looking at me. "You think so? Really?"

"It's possible. They were real operators, those two, you could see. They might've got hold of my pump, or pinched it themselves, and done a job on it, and just told him to give it back to me."

"Tracy."

"What?"

"You are not using your head."

"Why? We can't *know*—"

"Think, my little girl. Think. So he gives you the pump and you get your bike through the customs. Then what?"

Oh. Yeah. There was that.

"Well—" I was thinking, frantically now, because somehow in spite of everything I wasn't sure I wanted to drop Kev in the shit.

173

"Perhaps someone would've contacted him – or just nicked the pump, it wouldn't be hard – he wouldn't need to know—"

"Tracy, Tracy," Dad said, shaking his head.

More silence.

"Why you are trying so hard to get him from the hook?"

And then I was crying again, because, to say the true, I didn't know. I didn't like Kev any more, I was sure of that. But he was – I mean, when you thought of it – maybe he couldn't help it. His home-life and that, with his dad always out of work and the family for ever short of money. . . . Easy enough for me to say he was a louse and a rat. . . . I mean, if you'd *never* had enough, if you'd even been scared because your family was so hard pushed . . . everything you *are* comes from your background, all the programmes say that. What I mean is, was Kev responsible for what he'd done? Even if he was as big a bastard as it looked, was it all his fault?

Dad was sitting next to me now, holding me and listening while I tried to tell him all this. He lent me his hanky to blow my nose and when I'd said it all and calmed down a bit, he said:

"So now let us talk about Michael."

I looked up at him. Startled really. I'd half forgotten it was Michael who'd had to go and tell Dad.

"Tell me about that boy. What are *his* family situation?"

"Oh, awful. His dad's dead and his mum boozes—"

I stopped.

"So," said Dad, quiet. "Yet he is a very good boy. And his brother?"

"Yeah," I mumbled. "Darryl's okay."

"So it is not just families that decide," he said.

We sat in silence for a long, long time. Dad held my hand and I stared out of the window.

"Does Mum know?" I asked at last.

"They all know," Dad said.

"Is she in a state?"

"She was. Perhaps now not so bad."

"Does Vlady hate me?"

"Vlady could never hate you," Dad said, but then he had to say that, didn't he. "Why should anybody hate you? It was not your doing."

174

But Vlady would know that it was, in a way. I mean that I should have known. He always said I was only thick because I didn't want to use my head. All the clues were there, right from the off. I could read them now, like looking back and seeing lots of dirty great big road-signs, all lit up, that I hadn't even bothered to look at when I passed them. I'd just gone speeding on, head down. Vlady would've spotted them. Why should he let me off for not?

23 · Coming Home

You wouldn't believe there was worse to come, would you? But there was – in a way.

I mean, in another way nothing could have been worse than what happened to me at the customs in Harwich. Whenever I think of that I go all cold. But that was mainly physical. What happened when I got home was mental. Mental *torture*.

I'm not going to rehearse things ahead any more. It's useless. It never, never turns out anything like you imagine. I'd thought Dad would be the angry one, him being so strict and honest, and Mum, being Mum, would let me off and be sorry for me. Put the electric blanket on in my bed again, if you see what I mean – give me comfort. Be uncritical. But it wasn't like that.

The thing was, Dad believed what I told him. He thought I'd been thick (though he never said so) but that when you came down to it, it wasn't my fault. Vlady thought that too, though I took a fair bit of flak from him later. But Mum, and in their own ways Sean and Mary, took another view.

Mum saw the whole thing as a family disgrace. She never even asked herself whose fault it was, or if I could've helped it happening. All she knew was, she'd got a daughter who was going to come up in court for drug-smuggling, and probably get in the papers. She couldn't seem to see past that. She took the black view of everything. She thought Kev deserved worse than hanging for his part in it, but that didn't let me off, not in her eyes.

When we got home that night they were all sitting round the kitchen table, waiting. I almost heard them stop talking the minute the front door opened, and the whole house seemed to hold its breath while we walked the length of the corridor, down the two steps and into the room. Well, there's one thing – whatever that court-room's like, whatever the judge or whoever, says to me at the trial, it couldn't be worse than seeing the looks on my family's faces and hearing what they all had to say to me.

Mum looked as if she'd been crying her eyes out for hours. She picked her head up off her arms as I came in and stared at me like a mad woman. Her eyes were all red and glassy, and not just from tears – from rage.

"You *idiot!*" she cried out, straight off – only she said "eedjit". "You stupid, stupid, *stupid* girl! What have you done now, what have you brought on us? I always knew you'd go to the bad! Stubborn, wilful – changing the name we gave you, even, whoever heard of such a thing? With your crazy moods and tantrums, how else could it end but in disgrace?"

I wanted to turn and run away from her, from all of them, but Dad was behind me so I just stood. I looked away from Mum because I couldn't bear her eyes, and gave a quick look round at the others. Only Lily wasn't there. Mary was sitting by Mum, holding her hand and glaring at me. Sean had turned his chair till it was sideways on to me; he wasn't looking at me at all, just smoking hard and jigging one of his legs over the other. Vlady was standing up. His eyes were fixed on mine through his glasses. I gave him a look – I really cared more, in a way, what he thought than any of the others – begging him to say something to support me.

But it was Dad who spoke first. "It wasn't her fault," he said. "That Kevin, he put over one on her. She didn't know anything about it till the police dog—"

But Sean didn't let him finish.

"One look," he said, still with his head turned away, "just one look at that rotten little weasel face of his should have told her. *I* knew he was no good. I said—"

"You never!" I cried out, because Sean doesn't talk to me much and he'd certainly never said a word about Kev, for or against.

"Well, if I had, would you have listened? You never listen, you always think you know better. All the same, I knew."

"We all knew," said Mary.

"I didn't," said Vlady.

They all looked at him, even Sean.

"Easy enough to say now that you knew," Vlady said. "Half the people I look at look rotten to me; I don't judge by their faces. Anyway, she liked him, she was gone on him; nobody sees straight then." He blushed, but went on: "It's not people's faces you go by anyway, it's how they behave, how they treat you. We don't know how he treated her while they were away. Only she knows if he gave her any hints what he was up to."

Hints? Why did he have to say that? Of course there'd been hints, any amount of them. Sitting in that police station I'd made a list of them in my head, hadn't I. Vlady was right. Never mind Kev's face. If he'd stood in front of me two weeks ago and said, "Here, girl, I've got you in mind, I'm going to do a number on you, and have it off with you into the bargain", it couldn't have been much plainer – to anyone a little bit clever.

But luckily nobody got around to asking me direct, because Mum was all geared up. She'd had hours to build up a head of steam and now she had to let it all out on me. And when Dad tried to come to my rescue, that only made her worse.

"Ah sure, you'd take her side! She was always your darling! It was you let her go off to that God-forsaken Protestant pest-hole in the first place! Why could you not see that she went to a decent Catholic country if she had to be gallivanting off at all? At her age she should be at home, learning to look after a family! Not that any decent man'll have her, after this!"

There was a lot more of it before I was allowed to crawl away to bed. I felt like old Saint Sebastian, shot full of arrows. Only Mary hadn't said much. When we were in bed I started crying. I hadn't cried properly since Harwich and I needed to cry, howl even. I tried to keep it as quiet as I could, but it got on Mary's wick, and suddenly she had one of her flare-ups. She sat up in bed with a jerk and slammed her feet down on the floor.

"Shut up!" she said. "What you going on for? You never think of anybody but yourself, do you? You've always been the same, doing what you like, saying whatever comes into your head, and leaving me or someone else to cope."

"Like when?" I sniffed.

"Like when? When *not!* No doubt you've managed to forget that night a few weeks ago when you flounced out and were gone for hours! Who do you think picked up the bits of your plate and mopped the floor and calmed Mum down! Do you know how many times I've had to be nice to Lily after you've been rotten to her? And tonight just takes the cake. *Hours* I've sat with Mum, drying her tears and making her tea and telling her things weren't so bad – it's not the first time I've done it because of you, neither! And now look at you! What do you care that I've got to get up for work tomorrow? Snivelling away there, expecting me to be sorry for you – well, I'm not! Whether you knew what Kev was up to or not, a lot of it's your own fault. But you'll never admit it, not our Tracy, oh, no! And you'll make us pay your bills for you in the end, like you always have! Now I'm going to sleep downstairs and you can bawl your head off all night for all I care!"

And she dragged her bedding off her bed and stamped out, leaving me alone.

Like I said, Mary doesn't blow up often. So when she does, you have to take notice. I'd stopped crying out of shock at what she was saying, and I didn't start up again when she'd gone. I lay there on my back, thinking, *Is she right? Am I really like that?* Upsetting Mum and being mean to Lily and throwing tempers and leaving a trail of broken bits (not just plates) behind me for Mary, or Vlady, or Dad to pick up? Lying there in the dark I thought of a good few times, not just the Music Mill night, when I had. Made me feel as if all this business, now, was just a sort of highlight in my life's work as a misery-maker.

I tried to think about it properly but other things kept creeping in – stupid things, like that I hadn't given them their presents. When I thought of that, and how I'd planned to sit at the top of the table and tell them everything about our trip, and show them souvenirs, and make them laugh and go "oo-ah" at all my adventures – and then how it all ended – it was more than I could bear. One of the things Mum'd shouted at me was about the welcome-home meal she'd planned, my favourite foods and that, and how she felt like flinging them all through the window, that the stray cats deserved a treat better than I did. . . . I hated her, sort of, for saying that, for not taking my side and for making me feel so shitty. In the end I did start crying again. I cried myself to sleep.

Next day I'd stopped, but I didn't feel better. I felt worse. I didn't know what to do with myself. I didn't want to be at home. Lily was away, staying with Gran. I suspected Mum'd sent her on purpose, last night before I got back, to keep me from – I don't know – contaminating her or something. Sean was between jobs again, so he was around, but he was avoiding me. When I came into a room, he'd move out of it. That was his way of showing what he thought of me.

As for Mum, she wasn't speaking to me at all this morning. She fed me, but she didn't speak. She kept blowing her nose and sniffing as she did the housework, so I'd know she was crying. After a bit, every sniff was like a saw dragged across my nerves. Nobody could stick that for long, however they've deserved it.

I had breakfast on my own and then went back up to my room. I hadn't unpacked anything last night, so I started on that, to keep myself occupied. I pulled all the stuff out of my rucksack. It fell in a lump of clothes and food and presents and rubbish onto our bit of carpet. Lying right on top of the heap was that post-card I bought, of the *Destroyed City* man. I looked at him, all hollow, with no heart left in him. Despairing. . . . Well, I knew how he felt now all right. I stuck him up in the corner of the mirror, and if Mary didn't like him she knew what she could do.

Then I sorted out my dirty clothes, including the ones they'd thrown me out of that hotel for – they were half mouldy by now. What I'd normally have done, would be sling them all in the washing-machine for Mum to do. But I couldn't do that now. I just wanted to make myself invisible, not make work for her. So I washed them out myself in our hand-basin, using toilet soap. Then I carried them, and my sleeping-bag, down to hang on the line.

After that I meant to go back in and finish tidying up – all Mary needed from me was a mess all over the floor. But just as I was going, the back door opened and Sean came out for a smoke. The minute he saw me he turned right round and went back in. That made me burn inside. I wanted to rush after him and bang him with my fists and shout, "What's the matter, have I got plague or something? What kind of a brother are you anyhow?" But I knew that any kind of a row would only set me off crying again, and I'd made up my mind in the night that I'd cried all I was going to. For the moment, anyway.

Still, I couldn't go back in the house after that. So I went for a walk.

Trouble was, I didn't know where to go. Of course I wanted to see Michael, but he'd be at work probably, on the site, miles away. And I wanted to see Con in a way, but it's funny, there are times when it's your oldest friends you want. So I went to Karen's.

She lives in a block of flats near us. Not the tower blocks, the low, old-fashioned kind with curved balconies running all round. I climbed the steps to the third floor and rang her bell. Her mum opened the door.

"Oh," she said when she saw me. "It's you, Tracy. Well. You'd better come in."

No prizes for guessing what she thought of me. I'd have liked to turn and run – I couldn't take any more disapproval, not from anyone – but Karen had heard and she called me to go through into their living-room.

She was sitting there on the settee. With Cliff. She jumped up when I came in. He didn't move himself, of course. Didn't look at me either. Kept his nose in some magazine. They'd been having something to eat on plates, and some Pepsi. Karen's lipstick had all come off, whether from eating or kissing I couldn't be sure, but looking at Cliff I could guess. On again.

"Hallo, Trace, how are you?" she said, all bright. "They let you out, then?"

"Yeah," I said. "Did you think they'd lock me up straight away?"

She looked embarrassed. "Well, I didn't know, did I. We was all dead worried about you."

"*All* of you?"

"If you mean Kev, he wasn't on the train with us. He got an earlier one. You know, we all stayed with you till they made us go, and he'd bunked off by then, can you wonder?"

I suddenly imagined them rabbiting on about me all the way to Liverpool Street on the train. It made me curl up.

"What did you all think?" I asked. "I suppose you talked about nothing else on the way home."

"Yeah, well. . . ." She looked uncomfortable and kept trying to catch Cliff's eye but he wouldn't look at her. I could sense her mother, hanging about in the doorway behind my back, making signals at her. What signals? "Get her out of here," maybe. I was

181

feeling let down, something awful. I don't know what I'd expected – perhaps a hug from Karen, or her saying something right out about how she knew how I must be feeling and that they all knew I hadn't done it. . . . Instead she was moving things about on the table and looking as if she wished I'd go.

After a long silence she suddenly looked at me brightly and said, "Oh, by the way, guess what? Dad got tickets for *The Generation Game* tomorrow at the Bush. Me and Cliff's going."

I thought she must be going to ask me to come, or why mention it? But then I saw she only had two tickets and it was just something to say. She started on about how she couldn't wait to go and all that, but I interrupted.

"I suppose you think Kev and me was in it together."

"No! We don't, of course not, do we, Cliff?"

"I dunno what to think, do I," mumbled Cliff. "When I got all the facts, I'll tell you what I think. Till then I'm keeping well out of it."

"Oh well," I said, "if it's facts you want, you'd better come to my trial. You'll have to go back to Harwich for it. Bit further than the Bush, but it might be even more of a laugh than *The Generation Game*."

I hope I didn't *flounce* out, but I certainly brushed past Karen's mother without saying goodbye. And I seem to remember banging the flat-door a bit. Not hard. I was being very controlled, for me. But I was hurt. No denying that.

After that I had to test Con out, see if *she*'d gone all shifty-eyed about me. I walked fast through the streets to her house. The thought of Kev kept stabbing me like a blunt knife. He kept creeping into my thoughts and then I'd get this stab, and shove him out again. I felt I might be able to talk to Con about this feeling. *She* wasn't so gone on one of his pals that she wouldn't see my side clear. Not Con! Her own person, Con was. I knew that now, and I felt stupid for thinking Karen would be more help to me than Con would.

I almost ran up the path to her house and knocked, and rang the bell. I was impatient, waiting – I was mad to see her and get a bit of sense and comfort from her. But when the door finally opened, I got another shock.

It was her mum. I think I'd only seen her a couple of times

before – she never came to school functions and that, and now I saw why. She looked awful. She was very thin and even ugly, though you couldn't tell how she'd look if she'd only do herself up a bit. Her hair was half grey and straggly, and her clothes were all anyhow. Her hands were jumping all over the place, mostly around her face as if she was trying to hide it. No wonder. She'd got a black eye and her bottom lip was up like a damson. She'd been crying too, unless her eyes were red and watery naturally.

She looked at me, blank. "Yes?" she said, with a kind of gasp in her voice, like a hiccup.

"Is Con in?"

"Who?" she said. She really did, as if she'd never heard of her.

"Con."

"Oh! *Connie*. She's gone."

"Gone?" I said.

"Yes. In the night. She went. She said she'd go one day. Now she has."

"Where to?" I asked.

She started to cry again. She looked as if she was always on the edge of it, and the least thing would push her over.

"She's left us," she said. "I don't blame her. She couldn't stand it. She said if the rows didn't stop, she'd go." She leant against the doorpost and sobbed into both hands, her poor grey hair in rats'-tails on her neck.

It was horrible – my own disappointment, and being sorry for her on top. I didn't know what to do. I kind of put my hand on her shoulder and patted her. Without thinking I said what Dad would say:

"Can I help somesing?"

She shook her head, trying to stop herself crying. I looked over my shoulder. People were passing, looking up the path. I said, "Maybe you'd like to go inside." I looked past her into the dark hall. I could smell cats, and dirt. Who could wonder? Someone in that state couldn't clean the house – obviously. Still, I can't say I wanted to go in there with her, and I was relieved when she fished a hanky out of her sleeve and mopped up a bit and said, "Yes I will. But you run along, dear. It's Tracy, isn't it? Yes. Sorry I didn't know you at first. Connie talked about you. She thought a lot of you." She wiped her eyes and blew her nose and took a step backwards in the doorway.

"It's not so bad, you know," I said. "She'll come back to see you. When she's settled."

"Oh yes, I daresay," she said. "Better if she doesn't, in a way. Let her stop on her own and make her own life."

"Don't worry about her," I said. "She'll be okay."

She gave me a quick look. "You really think so?"

"Yeah, I do. She's strong."

"If she is," her mum said slowly, "I don't know where she gets it from."

We stood there, and I waited for her to go in and shut the door. It seemed unfeeling to walk away while she was standing there. But she seemed to have forgotten me. She just looked up at the sky with her eyes wide open. I remembered hearing that if you stare at the light after you've been crying, it stops your eyes being red. Maybe she was doing that, before her husband came home for his lunch (if he did) and saw the state she was in. . . . Rotten sod. But then maybe she drove him mad. . . . You never know about people's lives, what drives them to things.

"Never make judgements," Vlady said once. "You never really know."

Just the same, I made one. *Rotten sod.*

After a minute I said, "Goodbye then." I wanted to tell her to ask Con to ring me if she came back, but she was still staring at the sky and somehow I didn't want to disturb her.

24 · Butterflies

Once before – a long time ago, maybe five years – I'd gone to church by myself in the middle of the week.

It was because of something I'd done. The sort Mary was talking about. It started quite small, like most of the awful things. Me and Lily had been playing cards in the front room – I've forgotten what, Snap, or Beggar-My-Neighbour or some silly game. And Lily kept cheating. She cheated and cheated, and I tried everything to stop her doing it because I could feel myself getting wild inside, but she wouldn't. She just kept laughing and making this snortling noise in the back of her throat (she still does it sometimes when she wants to goad me) and at last I said I'd tell Dad. Dad would never let us cheat, even as a joke, and she knew she'd cop it if I did tell him. So she just picked up the pack of cards and flung them in my face.

I must have been half crazy already, because when I felt all those dozens of little jabs in my face from the card-corners, everything went red and black. I dived straight across the table at her and grabbed her by the neck.

Her chair went over backwards with us on top. I banged my head hard on the wall and I didn't even feel it. I had my hands round Lily's throat and I was choking her. *And it was lovely*. I'd have done for her, for sure – she was turning blue – if Vlady and Sean hadn't heard the row and come and dragged me off.

They had to revive Lil with cold cloths, and I got the only real hiding of my life from Dad. And I got the fright of my life, at least till this time. Because Lily was my little sister. I loved her when she wasn't driving me spare. And I could've killed her – I knew that. I'd always had a temper, but that was the first time I'd ever seen what it could lead to if I let it go.

I never did again, not like that. But it was there, that devil lurking inside me, deep down, waiting its chance. I felt it stirring now, as I walked away from Con's house, that monster that I'd seen a reflection of in Mum's eyes last night. It wasn't only an angry monster. It was a hate monster. My mum had hated me last night. *And I hated Kev this morning.*

Funny, it wasn't till my friends had let me down, one way or another, and I felt all alone, that I knew what I really felt about Kev. I don't know how it could be that I wasn't ready to shop him but that if he'd been there, in front of me, I'd have wanted to kill him. It made me feel sick, knowing how violent I could be, wanting to tear Kev in bits as if I could wipe the whole business out by wiping him out. So I did what I did that other time – I walked down the High Street and went into Our Lady of Lourdes.

It's nothing special, as churches go. All the coloured windows it had once were broken in the war, so now they're plain glass, which lets in lots of light. There's not a lot of atmosphere, like in some places. The altar's dead plain. There are about four statues, and some plaques round the walls showing the Stations of the Cross. That's about all. But there was a faint smell of old incense, and some candles lit round Our Lady's feet, and best of all it was familiar. I'd been coming there, Sundays, all my life. Only now it was different because it was only me.

I knelt down at the end of the pew where we usually tried to sit on Sundays, not too far forward in case Dad fell asleep. I said a few Hail Marys, to sort of catch Our Lady's attention, and then I talked to her and told her what had happened. It was a lot easier telling her than telling Dad, mainly because she knew all about it already. Even the part about wanting to kill Kev. I bet she knew the feeling.

Then I just sat there.

Funny, when we go to Mass and that, my mind wanders and I get bored very often, and wish it'd be over so we could go. Sitting there alone with nothing going on, I didn't get bored. I felt as if I could stay for ever.

I wasn't praying all the time, or even thinking. Just sitting. After a bit I felt like doing something, only without leaving the church. So I went up to the pulpit and there was the big Bible on its stand, open at last Sunday's lesson. I read it, but it didn't say much to me. So I turned the big, heavy pages back a bit until I saw, at the top of a page, the words *Lamentations of Jeremiah*. I liked the sound of that, it suited my mood. I shut my eyes and put my finger on a verse, and believe it or not this was it:

She weepeth sore in the night, and her tears are on her cheeks: among all her lovers she hath none to comfort her: all her friends have dealt treacherously with her, they are become her enemies.

I must've read that verse ten times.

Don't ask me why it made me feel so much better, but it did. Perhaps because every now and then you can't help wondering if maybe it's all just superstition and there's no one up there. But if I wasn't directed to open the Bible there, and put my finger just on that verse, out of all the thousands, well, how could it happen? It proved something to me. That I hadn't just been chatting away to myself, down there in the pew.

And if I'd needed any more proof, it came as I was walking home. It wasn't knocking-off time and he lived the other side of Acton, but there he was – Michael – coming towards me in the precinct. As if he knew where I'd head for. Or maybe he was heading there himself.

I was so glad to see him! I wanted to run to him, but I just stood still and let him come to me.

"Hallo, Tracy."

"Hallo," I said. I was blushing but I was so brown perhaps it didn't show.

"Been to church?" he said, as if it was the most ordinary thing in the world to go to church on a Wednesday morning.

"Yeah."

"How'd you feel today?"

"A bit better. Not much. I wanted to thank you."

"What for?"

"Everything. And – coming to tell my family. That must've been horrible for you."

"I nearly funked it. I just stood the other side of your front hedge and I was shaking all over. I don't know how I made myself do it."

"I don't either. I couldn't have, in your place."

"I thought of you in Harwich, waiting," he said. He wasn't looking at me, he was looking across the street, and following every passing car with his eyes.

"What happened? Who opened the door?"

"Your brother – not the one with glasses, the other one. I

187

asked to see your dad, and he took me into the kitchen. And they were all there, your little sister too, and they looked at me. They'd been expecting you back. And I suppose I looked. . . . Anyway your mum jumped up at the sight of me and started yelling, 'Holy God, what's happened?' or something like that, so I couldn't mess about, I had to tell them straight out."

"They all heard? Even Lily?"

"Yeah. I'm sorry. I didn't think till later I should have talked just to your parents. I'm sorry."

I dragged up a deep sigh, like one of Dad's. "You couldn't help it. They had to know."

We stood there for a bit, watching the cars as if they were dead fascinating. I felt Michael touching my hand, and I moved closer to him.

"You mustn't be worried," he said.

"Oh, no, of course not!" I said, sarcastic.

"No," he said. "I mean it. You've nothing to worry about. You'll get off."

"It's heroin," I said. I hadn't dared even think it till now.

"I don't care if it's a ton of Dioxin," he said. "You'll get off."

"You can't be sure," I said. "You can't even be sure I didn't have anything to do with it. *You* never saw him give me back that pump – he made sure nobody saw that."

"If it's a matter of witnesses," he said, "I know you'd lost it, and I know you got it back. But it won't depend on that. It'll depend on Kev telling them the truth."

"He won't."

"If you're so sure of that," he said, "I wonder you went with him in the first place."

"I didn't know him then, did I."

"Maybe you should've taken a closer look."

"Stop talking like my brother Vlady."

"The one with glasses?"

"Yeah."

"He's okay, I like him. He was the first one to start talking sense last night, saying you'd need a lawyer and that he betted you wasn't to blame—"

"Did he?"

188

"He wanted to come up with your dad to get you, but he said he had to go on his own."

We stopped talking for a bit and just walked. I even managed to stop thinking.

My head seemed to have emptied itself down my arm and into my fingers. I was almost living down there, in my hand where it was touching his. It was like the relief of going to sleep, only better. I was even happy.

But suddenly I woke up. Because I saw where we were walking. Straight onto the railway bridge, where my paint-writing was – my graffiti. I wanted to drag him away so he wouldn't see it. But that'd be a dead give-away. So I let him walk me towards it, just hoping and praying he wouldn't notice.

Who could help noticing? There were the words, glaring at us in the sun. Michael looked at them – and stopped.

"Look at that," he said.

"Oh yeah!" I said, as if I'd never seen it before.

He smiled at me. "I didn't do it, Officer," he said. "I swear! That's not to say I don't agree with it, though."

Then his eyes narrowed. "Now I wonder," he said, "who knew him well enough to write that! Someone who can't spell, that's for sure."

"Spoils the bridge, doesn't it."

"Not much to spoil . . . ugly old thing. Still. If you wanted to get it off, we might try the same technique I used on poor old Erasmus."

"But this is paint."

"We might try, some dark night," he said. "Then, when we'd done the job and got it all cleaned off, I might write something instead. I used to be good at love-hearts when I was younger."

I stared at him. "*You* used to write on walls?"

"I did a lot of things a few years ago I wouldn't think of doing now," he said. "But anyway there's things you don't want to advertise. These days I keep my love-hearts for February the fourteenth."

I took this in slowly, because I was thinking more of something else. It was only later I thought what he really meant.

"Michael, why – how are you so sure I'll get off?"

"I told you. Kev'll do the necessary."

"You don't know him."

"And you do, I suppose?"

"Well enough to know he'd see me rot before he'd land himself in the cart."

"That just goes to show, don't it? Because he's already done it."

He said it so casual I thought he must be having me on.

"What do you mean? How do you know?"

"That's what I was coming to tell you. I didn't go in to work this morning, I went to see Kev. I thought he might make trouble, but not a bit of it. He was like a lump of jelly, just waiting for someone to come and tell him what to do. You think you had a bad night? He had a worse one. I think he was expecting your brothers to come and do him in! He was so relieved it was only me that he let me trot him down to the station straight away. Left him on the doorstep to go in and say his piece."

*

Kev's confession hasn't got me right off the hook. The police thought he might be covering up for me, so I've still got to go to court, but the Chief Inspector at Harwich has let Dad know that there's a good chance I won't be charged. Or if I am, and there's still a case, it doesn't look too bad for me.

It wasn't the end of it in the family, though. There's still a lot of bad feeling. Vlady took it hard, somehow. He said, "*We* should've gone and settled with that little bastard; she's our sister." Dad said he wouldn't have let them. He says you have to trust the processes of law and justice – perhaps because he's a foreigner, Dad still believes that the British police and courts and that can never be wrong.

Sean says he *would* have gone, and beaten Kev to a pulp, if he'd been sure enough that I hadn't had some part in what happened. It's hard to love a brother like that, but I suppose I'll get back to loving him – maybe around next Christmas, when we're playing our football game in the park.

When Lily came home she said Gran never doubted me and neither did she. But then, neither of them was caught up in the atmosphere of that first awful night when *nobody* was sure. Mary was nice. She apologised. She said she'd only been against me because she'd had Mum raving and crying on her hands for five hours before I got home. Well, I can understand that.

But Mum was the odd one. I couldn't make her out at first, after she heard about Kev going to own up. I could tell there was trouble between her and Dad. She didn't look anyone in the eye and she still went around the house sniffing and blowing her nose.

But then a couple of days later she came up to my room where I was sitting. She actually knocked before she came in, a thing she's never done in her life.

"Tracy—"

"'Lo, Mum."

"Can I come in?"

"What's to stop you?"

She came in and sat on the bed.

"What are you doing?"

"Writing."

"What, a letter is it?"

"No." I hesitated. "I'm trying to write down – about our trip and that – and how it all happened."

She looked down at her hands in her lap. She tried to say something but somehow it stuck.

"Would you like to read it when I've finished?" I asked. I was surprised to hear myself offer that – five minutes ago I'd have said I'd die before I'd show it to her, any of it. (I still haven't and maybe I won't, I don't know if I could show it to anybody yet.)

Mum looked up. She had tears in her eyes – *again*: I was getting fed up to the back teeth with her crying all the time, but now she looked so pitiful I felt myself melt.

"Yes," she said. "All except the last part. Have you come to the last part yet?"

"No, not yet."

"Are you telling the truth about everything?"

"Yeah. Not much point otherwise."

"You always had a gift," she said quietly. "Don't be too hard on me when you do come to the last part."

And suddenly I saw she'd come to make it up with me. And I jumped up and went to her and hugged her and she hugged me back (she doesn't hug any of us much; she shows how she feels by doing things for us) and said, "We'll have it tonight, the welcome-home meal. I must go and do the potatoes." And she got up quickly and went out, closing the door behind her.

I felt so choked up after that I couldn't get on with the writing, so I thought I'd get my presents wrapped nicely, ready for the evening when I could give them out – I'd even give Sean his, though not with a very good feeling. I got them out of the drawer where I'd hidden them wrapped up in one of my T-shirts. And as I unrolled that, I saw something pinned to it. It was the filigree butterfly Michael had bought me in Holland.

I unpinned it and looked at it. It was so beautiful. I sat with it on my hand, just admiring it. If I moved my fingers under it, it was easy to pretend it was alive.

After a bit I took it to the dressing-table. I had one of the two little drawers and Mary had the other. Mary's is always tidy and mine's always a mess. I opened mine to put my butterfly away, and there, right in the middle of all the jumble, was another one.

Another butterfly. A cheap little imitation gold one with some glittery stones for eyes and shiny blue paint smeared on its wings. Now where had that come from? Then I remembered – of course. It was the one Kev gave me, that he got out of the grab-machine that first time we went out together.

I held the two of them side by side. The hand-made silver one, only one exactly like it in the world – and the imitation one, that they turn out thousands of in Hong Kong. Easy to see when they were together like that – easy to see the real difference. The same difference there was in the givers.

I wrapped the silver one up so it wouldn't get tarnished and put it in a box by itself in the front of my drawer. And I threw the other one away.

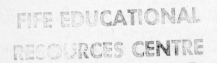